CW00540572

Also by F

THE
MAGICAL
SHIELD

About the Author

Frater U.∴D.∴ (Belgium), founder of Pragmatic and Ice Magic, is Europe's best known practical magician and contemporary occult author. He has written more than twenty-five books. Among his translations are the books of Peter Carroll and Ramsey Dukes, and Aleister Crowley's *Book of Lies*.

To Write to the Author

If you wish to contact the author or would like more information about this book, please write to the author in care of Llewellyn Worldwide, and we will forward your request. Both the author and publisher appreciate hearing from you and learning of your enjoyment of this book and how it has helped you. Llewellyn Worldwide cannot guarantee that every letter written to the author can be answered, but all will be forwarded. Please write to:

Frater U.∴D.∴
℅ Llewellyn Worldwide
2143 Wooddale Drive
Woodbury, MN 55125-2989

Please enclose a self-addressed stamped envelope for reply, or $1.00 to cover costs. If outside the USA, enclose an international postal reply coupon.

FRATER U∴D∴

THE
MAGICAL
SHIELD

Protection Magic to
Ward Off Negative Forces

Llewellyn Worldwide
Woodbury, Minnesota

Originally published © 2015 by Ansata Verlag, München, Part of Random House Group GmbH

Originally edited by Juliane Molitor

FIRST U.S. EDITION
Fourth Printing, 2021

Book design by Bob Gaul
Cover illustration by Thomas Reinert, Reinert & Partners, Munich, Germany
Editing by Laura Graves
Figures 1–4 and 8 by Thomas Reinert
Figures 5–7 by Llewellyn art department
Figure 9 by Hagen von Tulien

Llewellyn Publications is a registered trademark of Llewellyn Worldwide Ltd.

Library of Congress Cataloging-in-Publication Data
Names: U∴D∴, Frater, 1952– author.
Title: The magical shield : protection magic to ward off negative forces / Frater U∴D∴.
Other titles: Magische Schutzschild. English
Description: First U.S. Edition. | Woodbury : Llewellyn Worldwide, Ltd, 2016. | Includes bibliographical references.
Identifiers: LCCN 2016029376 | ISBN 9780738749990
Subjects: LCSH: Protection magic.
Classification: LCC BF1623.P75 U1513 2016 | DDC 133.4/3—dc23
LC record available at https://lccn.loc.gov/2016029376

Llewellyn Worldwide Ltd. does not participate in, endorse, or have any authority or responsibility concerning private business transactions between our authors and the public.

All mail addressed to the author is forwarded, but the publisher cannot, unless specifically instructed by the author, give out an address or phone number.

Any Internet references contained in this work are current at publication time, but the publisher cannot guarantee that a specific location will continue to be maintained. Please refer to the publisher's website for links to authors' websites and other sources.

Llewellyn Publications
A Division of Llewellyn Worldwide Ltd.
2143 Wooddale Drive
Woodbury, MN 55125-2989
www.llewellyn.com

Printed in the United States of America

Contents

Foreword

The protection of one's own physical, mental, and spiritual integrity has always been a fundamental component of old as well as new survival and cultural technologies: Primordial shamanism, the god and demon cults of Sumer and Egypt, the yoga practices of Indian Vedic culture, the culture of the Taoist martial arts rooted in China and Southeast Asia, the mystery schools of Greco-Roman antiquity, the hermetic ceremonial magic of the Renaissance and its renewed formation in the nineteenth and twentieth centuries, the New Thought movement, positive thinking—they all deal in detail with the magical protection of humanity.

In a completely different context, the more secular disciplines have applied themselves to this subject since their inception. From psychology to the social sciences, from anthropology, cognitive psychology and applied neurology to the more pragmatic areas of success and management coaching—the same question is always foremost: How does a person function on their own and in a social setting, and what must they do to weather life's challenges successfully?

This work goes into the basics of Western and Eastern survival disciplines; namely the three fundamental levels of human existence: body, mind, and soul. The concept will be communicated through easily comprehensible and undemanding instructions and practices. The emphasis is on the practical application of old—and yet ever new, all the same—spiritual and anthropological knowledge.

What follows is an unconventional approach to a genuinely integrated everyday model of protection, still proven to be extremely powerful.

Fra U∴D∴
Vbique Daemon Vbique Devs

1

THE HUMAN BEING— THE MOST FRAGILE MODEL OF SUCCESS IN EVOLUTION

Our Strengths, Our Weaknesses, and Our "Self-inflicted Immaturity"—An Appraisal

You don't have to continue referring to the "Crown of Creation" to pay appropriate tribute to humanity and its place in nature. It is beyond dispute that humanity should be recognized as the epitome of evolution's success. No other species has come anywhere as close to bringing the planet so comprehensively under its control as the human race has. It really doesn't matter that in the hit parade of successful life forms, rivals emerge that could be taken seriously purely in a numerical sense, for example insects, bacteria, or viruses. To a great extent they might even be better equipped for survival. It is said that there are certain species of insects that would even live through a nuclear war, something that humanity could barely hope to do. However, we have stamped our mark upon the earth. Our level of influence has reached so far that we, in the truest sense of the word, could utterly obliterate our home planet overnight; a thing that most of us probably agree would be a rather dubious achievement.

For sure, there are arguments over when exactly human development began, whether it was fifty thousand or two million years ago. That is merely a question of definition and of one's particular academic method of approach. All the same, it cannot be denied that humanity is without a doubt anything but all-powerful and invulnerable. There have in fact already been several evolutionary biologists who have maintained that the survival of humanity is more than a little bit surprising, as the human being is actually quite a fragile creature. Even though it has proved itself to be eminently adaptable—to the deserts of Africa, the Asian steppes, and the ice fields of the Arctic—humanity also requires a very finely balanced environment. Just a half percent more or less nitrogen in the earth's atmosphere and it could all look quite different. No one knows for sure what would happen to the human project it if actually came to a pole shift, which has certainly taken place several times already in the earth's history. Today's concerns about the ways and means in which we collectively but also individually treat our environment are more than a passing fad. It might take a long time for humanity to become fully aware of its dependencies and to have an inkling that the flipside of the "progress fetish" that has so fervently gripped us since the Enlightenment and the subsequent Industrial Revolution has within itself the potential capacity for failure, which might not be described as merely a low-level "industrial accident," if it manifests itself in the entire species' complete extinction.

Environmental disasters such as droughts and the desertification of previously fertile and arable land, earthquakes, volcanic eruptions, tsunamis, meteor strikes, global warming, high levels of radiation—could these kinds of things not perhaps start on a smaller scale? Yes, indeed they can, and thus we arrive at the actual theme of this book. Many people become involved in environmental protection and campaigning for peace, fighting for the maintenance of human rights and for greater democracy. I am not demeaning or slighting any of this here in any form whatsoever. Unfortunately, it seems we have let go of the awareness that we only have command over limited and very straightforward energies and skills, and that it's not just our planet, our society, the people of other countries and continents and also the various ideological, sexual, and religious minorities who need our increased attention—but also ourselves!

It is in fact a truism one hardly dares say out loud: If we don't treat ourselves with care either by taking advantage of our strengths or by allowing for our weaknesses and not just ignoring our vulnerabilities in the interests of some kind of "higher cause," our effort sooner or later suffers a sharp set-back at best, perhaps through an accident or a sudden illness, which we might only get over successfully with some effort. Or the abrupt ending follows, death itself, which in our culture we attempt to block so diligently. What is perhaps still more important: Only when we treat ourselves well are we in a position to care for others and participate successfully in making the world a better place. And even if we have no such lofty ambitions and might not care too much about the world around us because we have enough problems to deal with anyway, it's left to us to grasp that it is only the careful stewardship of ourselves that provides the well-founded hope that whatever it is we are pursuing as our life's goal actually comes within our reach.

You don't need to be some heartless egotist to give space to the fact that we must put our own house in order in the first place before we preoccupy ourselves with some other matter extending beyond it. It's actually just like building a house. Firstly, the foundations must be in place for us to be able to erect a stable structure upon them so the whole thing won't come crashing down after the slightest earth tremor. Applying this to the biological field, it means nothing less than ensuring the continuation of our existence. To that end, our basic external requirements have to be met for us to serve our own needs adequately from the start. In other words, the basis of all existence is secured space, a set of surroundings that will help ward off danger, or, more abstractly expressed, protection. In terms of linguistic history, the German word *Schutz* (English: protection) is derived from the Middle High German *schützen*, which originally referred to the damming or confinement of water. There is also a relationship to the Middle Low German *schütten* meaning to stop up, imprison, or ward off, as well as to the Old English *scyttan*, whence we get "shut" in modern English. In addition, it is related to the Middle High German *schüten*, which means to pile up, churn up, or retain earth, from which the current meaning of guarding or making secure derives.

So we are dealing with fending off dangers and threats from outside with determination. Whether we refer to bodies of water carrying the threat of drowning, beasts of prey, or even worse, human enemies. Only when we keep in mind before what and against what we truly must protect ourselves to survive once and for all, and in total sobriety will it become genuinely apparent to us how fragile our human existence is. Whether it be quite concrete and tangible elements and factors like thieves, rapists, vengeful ex-partners, pathogenic organisms, drunk drivers, fraudsters, roofs at risk of collapse, potholes, rabid dogs, unstable furniture, icy sidewalks, slippery stairs, pitfalls, rickety scaffolding, defective brakes—or whether it's a question of more abstract and less tangible threats like workplace intrigue, malicious gossip, false accusations in the courtroom, depression and emotional instability, betrayal, breach of trust, self-doubt, psychological abuse, humiliation, miscalculations, despair, terror, horror, anxiety disorders, addictive behavior, oppression, enslavement, or death threats. It doesn't take much imagination to extend this list; it could fill up entire volumes.

Whoever has committed themselves to the spiritual path will encounter a whole additional batch of problems and dangers that can threaten peace of mind or even nullify every hope of enlightenment, salvation, or liberation no matter the metaphysical aims they are pursuing. Whether it's the vexatious principle of karma, a concept Hinduism and Buddhism have bestowed upon the world; the exceedingly richly embellished canon of sinfulness owed to the monotheistic Judaism, Christianity, and Islam; the "Dark Night of the Soul," the terror of all the mystics, not to mention the Qliphoth of the Kabbalists, to name but a few, it's in the nature of the mysteries, that their true secrets can only be experienced but not reliably communicated. And so there will remain across this vast terrain many a tripwire, many a misunderstanding, many a self-destructive extravagance, and many a delusional structure it's essential for us to protect ourselves against.

Paradigms of the Human Condition

If you have been reading carefully, you will probably have noticed that we have followed a threefold classification in this listing of dangers that threaten life, existence, and health, which follows the classical division of people into body, mind, and soul. This is a widespread organizational convention that has characterized the Western image of the human being for several hundred years. By convention, one understands the agreement established across most of society as a whole concerning basic concepts; avenues of approach; social, moral, or ethical norms; classification techniques; methodologies; and the like. This note is important because it helps us keep in mind that conventions are based solely on common consensus and don't necessarily have to have anything to do with reality or truth. Even if a culture intends to see something like "objectivity" according to certain conventions, this does not have to apply any more than that to another culture. And whoever is not aware of this will have major difficulties in grasping and adequately appreciating the ways of thinking and seeing in other foreign conventions and cultures.

The same applies in this case. Body-mind-soul is just one of many possible models of the human species, and before we deal with it in more detail, justification is needed for why we prefer this to other models. Incidentally, we have to deal on an almost daily basis with a very widespread variant on this model—namely that the scientific portrait of humans, represented in science, research, technology, medicine (and even politics and economics) categorically refuses to include the soul, indeed ignoring its existence. It is not the same as explicitly denying it altogether (as for example materialism does) but it does illustrate a refusal to engage with its possible or held to be impossible existence. Since the Enlightenment and the ideological and social upheavals it generated, we have learned that metaphysics and consequently religion too are held to be private matters needing neither state nor general society's involvement. Unfortunately, the result has been bloody wars of faith and religious persecutions dragged on for hundreds if not thousands of years. Since the tail end at least of the nineteenth century, the concepts of the state and of democracy in the West have been informed by the exclusion of religious and metaphysical matters and all those sorts of questions that at their core are "otherworldly" and thus point to the realm of the private. That was by no means always so, and as contemporary Islam shows as an example, it has not been the case for every culture on our planet for a long time either. The bottom line is this: such a model doesn't have to be mandatory for all people in equal measure, and it certainly isn't objective.

In the Western history of thought are several alternative models on offer, including that of Theosophy. Here we get involved in a somewhat complicated variety of different "bodies" having completely different functions that correspond to a series of hierarchically arranged stages of existence and development. In addition to the physical body are the etheric body, the astral body, and the Buddhi body, to name a few. If we add to that the theory of reincarnation (familiar in the West since ancient times but most likely borrowed from Eastern teachings), the image of humanity becomes even more complicated. In the concept of metempsychosis, conceived from ancient Greek metaphysics, is a kind of evolutionary theory that long precedes Charles Darwin: the individual soul works its way up through various animal forms until it reaches the human. Should some kind of development take place during the process, of course the next question is: What does the concept of "soul" actually mean? This obviously also applies to all the various Eastern reincarnation theories. In general, it is assumed that the physical body is only the vehicle or the temporary housing for the subtle soul. This has in itself a far greater significance than the world, understood to be *Maya* or "illusion." In most Vedic philosophies, the soul is a splitting-off or an emanation of the divine evolving via the cycle of birth, death, and rebirth before ascending to reunite with the divine, different from its original form in Buddhism. Here the Vedic concept of *Atman* is utterly rejected, seen in the cultural context of the time as an enormous break with the traditional theory of being; it has quite rightly been called the "Buddhist Revolution." There is, however, even in Buddhism in its original form a clear place for the theory of reincarnation. What actually reincarnates according to the early Buddhist outlook is merely karma, not the individual's soul.

Following the arc of reincarnation back to the West, we can observe across the various epochs a variety of religious and philosophical currents that have been designated in academic circles (more wrongly than rightly) Gnosis, or Gnosticism. To say nothing about the detailed differences, most Gnostic schools and movements did at least agree on one thing, that the core essence of a human being consists of a "divine spark," a piece of the substance of that faraway primal God—who is not responsible for this creation—needing to be rescued from the outrageous world of demiurgic creation into the realm of Pleroma ("fullness"). As the contemporary source material doesn't allow for overly precise statements, unfortunately, we can only speculate to what extent we can attribute the same or similar qualities to this "divine spark" as we can to the concept of "soul," the latter of which has prevailed via the later Christian church. Here again we have to note straight away that we are dealing with a differently formulated picture of humanity from the one that is likely to be more familiar today. Whoever's head is not already spinning might pose themselves the naïve question: Which is correct? This is exactly the sort of thing that can be qualified through the use of the term "convention," but—and this is more important—it will certainly then be dealt with more easily.

It was Maximilien de Robespierre—held in ill repute by the history books until this day—who in a speech to the Welfare Committee of the French Revolution formulated the saying: "Truth is what benefits the people." This definition might grate on you, you can condemn it as malicious, defame it as heartless and technocratic, declare it to be stupid and good for nothing—and all this will go on happening again and again. As with most of Robespierre's thoroughly interchangeable ideologemes, this is also an example of an exaggeration of the philosophy of Jean-Jacques Rousseau, whose concept of a social contract we still pay homage to today. Clearly, this statement makes one point above all others: everything we generally understand as reality or truth is the expression of a convention—thus the consequence of a collective agreement—we here will consider without question to be a socialization or an acculturation.

Practical usage has its advantages, and we will explore it in greater detail. To start, a brief note should suffice: In using the methods and practices presented here, you don't have to commit yourself to any kind of ideological, spiritual, or philosophical direction. Likewise, you are free to stick with your own beliefs and convictions, whatever you may prefer. Consider the approach presented here as a suggestion that can be modified according to your own discretion. You are also free to reject it or simply adopt it. It is certainly not the case that you should commit to any particular worldview or believe in whatever some preacher, missionary, or guru sells to you as the last word in wisdom. That said, it is always advisable—and we will continue to emphasize this during the course of these instructions—to question all positions critically and test them out on the basis of whether they are compatible with your individual life experience, your understanding of the world, and your personal level of development. This applies to what is presented here as well as to those beliefs and insights ingrained a long time ago; everything is done in accordance with the way you orient and shape your life. If a multitude of regularly divergent interpretations and explanatory models are used here, it is by no means being done to confuse you—quite the opposite. Only this broad spectrum of possibilities will allow you to arrive at a modus operandi that's really useful to you as opposed to running the risk of limiting yourself through old and cherished but unreflective dogmas, prejudices, and assumptions.

In the following, we would first like to clarify several terms and discuss spiritual-intellectual and practical tools and learning models, before we go into how you can best work with the procedures presented in the next chapter.

Body

The term "body" refers to what is tangible in you and manifests materially. It is the purely biological component of your existence: a highly complex structure of bone, flesh, skin, connective tissue, blood vessels, inner and outer organs, and so on. It is of a material nature, and like all matter, is subject to the laws of nature, created through procreation, pregnancy, and childbirth, of a finite existence therefore destined eventually to die and disintegrate, and thus to dissolve back again into its constituent parts. The body undergoes an evolution beginning with the infant who is totally reliant on its environment, to the toddler who has already become independent to a limited extent, the adolescent, up to the adult, who manifests the highest attainable degree of autonomy until the process of aging and decay (to say nothing of illnesses) reduces everything again. In extreme cases, freedom of movement and ability to care for oneself will at some point go completely, and ultimately death brings an end to the whole system.

Western history and its ideas treated the body with contempt for a long period of time as the mere "prison of the soul." It was finally during the Renaissance and the Enlightenment that followed when we managed to free ourselves from that outlook handed down by Christian dogma. The wane of the notion that the "body is nothing, the soul is everything," meant that we could then devote ourselves to the study of anatomy on a wider scale and finally bring to fruition all that we understand today about medicine and human physiology. There is little doubt that a large proportion of the knowledge relating to the human body we have amassed up to now owes itself to a secular, sometimes even outspokenly anti-clerical and religion-averse point of view and procedural approach, one that generally prevails even today in Western-oriented science.

This observation is significant for several reasons. Firstly, it makes it clear that to start, humanity must free itself from the fundamental fatalism of the earlier religious way of understanding in order to dedicate itself to a more sober approach that focuses on pure objectivity and also on what is factual and quantifiable instead of continuing to rely upon purely speculative and not objectively verifiable assertions, for example that illnesses are a punishment from God or are attributable to possession by some evil spirits.

Not that these kinds of simplistic speculations are entirely a thing of the past. Nowadays our paths cross more frequently with some Christian or Islamic cleric who while often very media-savvy will explain away diseases like AIDS or ebola, or natural disasters like earthquakes or storm surges as divine punishment for the supposedly sinful lives of human beings and their "moral brutalization."

On the other hand, the demystification of the corporeal set in motion by the Enlightenment was bought at the cost of a radical overthrow of the hitherto prevailing view of a harmonious universe. It is especially evident in the philosophy of materialism, where we encounter exclusively material forms of existence and are told that all mental phenomena can be conceived as purely material via the slogan "existence determines consciousness." This view is also consistent with the ideologically somewhat earlier held mechanistic worldview that outlined merely a kind of clockwork mechanism that was believed to prevail both in the universe and the human body.

Here, then, a clear separation emerges: this is a world of matter, clearly existing and operating independently of everything else and in particular of any sort of postulated mental or even spiritual factors. If there is any creator or greater "plan" for this world of matter, be it the absolute existences of spiritual essences or whether human beings have souls or not—in this context it doesn't interest us at all. There is a sharp line drawn between measurable—"objectifiable"—facts and factors, and the merely asserted and postulated—defined as "purely speculative"—elements. On the level of civic philosophy and politics, this notion is reflected in the radical separation between church and state, as it still stands in the West even to this day on the list of demands of the secular, anti-clerical, agnostic, and atheist interest groups. In principle, there would probably be nothing here to complain about either, in as much as this approach actually satisfies their own demands, namely to explain or to cover without exception everything challenging and not yet understood in the medical field—that is to say, illnesses and their healing or prevention.

As I have already indicated, this objectifiable/speculative view has until now held firmly and fundamentally in the sciences; modern medicine continues to be founded on it. All the same, since the end of the nineteenth century there have been constant promptings for a root-and-branch revision of this vulgar-materialist model of explanation. The discovery of the psyche and thus the spiritual (at least in the non-religious sense of the word) has usually been attributed to Sigmund Freud and his psychoanalysis. Yet although Freud's achievements in this field are undeniable, he did have his precursors. The best known of these was Anton Mesmer, who in the events leading to the French Revolution was already popularizing his concept of "animal magnetism," celebrated frenetically in the salons of Europe. All the while, he did not achieve that much except employ a variant on the hypnosis techniques that had been known since ancient times and demonstrated its therapeutic use to the public. Nevertheless, his influence on human understanding in Europe can hardly be overstated.

Mesmer's success can't just be explained by the fact that he was clearly a brilliant showman and crowd favorite, who was impeccably aware of how to sell himself. His charisma probably wouldn't have brought him too much in the long run had he not also caught the spirit of the times by making it apparent that bodily processes could allow themselves to be influenced by means of psycho-emotional techniques and practices. Up to that point it was widely assumed for centuries (meaning since the end of the Middle Ages) that the human body was more or less an autonomous, machine-like apparatus, albeit one that is dependent upon environmental influences, nutrition, heat, cold, etc., and whose well-being could be controlled at best through external means such as medicines, water cures, warm baths, and similar influences. Hypnosis was well known to the ancients, including probably Egypt. Mesmer's unique achievement was that he was able to convince his contemporaries that the body is not simply a completely isolated mechanism resistant to spiritual and psychological influences. He also gave people a fairly plausible explanation by spreading the idea of animal magnetism as an all-pervasive vital force, availing himself of it using "magnetizing" physical movements and "magnetic baths" in tubs filled with magnetized iron filings. All this seemed very convincing to his contemporaries and was accordingly taken up enthusiastically. He proved a most persistent thorn in the side of the orthodox medical practitioners of his day. They accused him of charlatanism and used all their power to fight him but could only have a small effect on his mass appeal.

Ultimately, it was left to Sigmund Freud and his band of disciples to change the Western picture of humanity on an enduring basis and to broaden the dimensions of the psychic (as well as the psychological). Even if neither Freudian nor Jungian depth psychologies were able to establish themselves formally as sciences, they can't be dismissed any longer in the world of contemporary therapy. Therapies too follow trends and styles, and psychology was no exception. It was almost an expectation in the lives of media professionals, actors, and producers in Hollywood and New York in the 1950s and 1960s to undergo psychoanalysis on a regular basis. That focus might have shifted somewhat today, however. In contrast, psychotherapeutic methods and treatment services today are more tightly integrated into everyday public health. Granted, the old dispute between pharmacology—and neurology-based psychiatry and behaviorism—and clinical empiricism-based psychology—which may have to be disengaged from the fundamental assumptions of Freud, Jung, or Adler—still informs our contemporary confrontation with psychically related disturbances and illnesses. It cannot be denied that we no longer see the human body as an isolated matter-based machine even if the "soul-based"—psychology's territory (after all, "psychotherapy" translates as "care of the soul")—might have no connection with the religious or metaphysical concept of the primordial human essence.

Of course, it's still easy to distinguish a hip fracture from an auto-aggressive personality disorder, a fact also reflected in various different therapeutic approaches. However, when it comes to the matter of the optimization of the healing process, for example as regards the aforementioned bone fracture, any physician will pretty swiftly move into psychological territory. Thus it could by all means be the case that a good attending physician will not only prescribe the appropriate medication and rehabilitation procedures but will also include perhaps the family of the person concerned and will give them advice on ways of handling the patient, such as paying increased attention, visiting with children or grandchildren, constructive ways of speaking with them, encouragement, and so on, to optimize the healing process.

It would be an exaggeration to claim that the pendulum might swing back completely the other way after the excesses of a rather mechanistically formulated materialism and positivism to a view that has been purported in Western philosophy and metaphysics since Plato; namely that the spirit or the "idea" lies as the basis of all existence and has an enduring effect on it. Yet the consequent relativization is unmistakable. To a not inconsiderable degree, the research required by a rigorous, objective scientific approach has served to make it

essential to pay greater attention to the psychological components of humanity in the interest of optimizing the art
of healing. The results of placebo research have at the very
least put into question a large proportion of pharmacology's
scientific assumptions. Cases of self-healing or "remission"
(to use the medical term) have attracted enough interest to
fund research. In any case, the understanding of physical
processes must be supplemented by the inclusion of psychological processes and mechanisms because the purely mechanistic approach in everyday practice has proved much too
limited, resulting in prescriptions and treatments suboptimal
or completely ineffectual.

If we are speaking here about "body," we must next go
past the definition given earlier and incorporate psychological factors as well, in particular emotional states, plus that
which has been described to this day (for want of a better
definition and more poorly than well) as "consciousness," to
say nothing of the un- or subconscious occurrences within
the human organism. For the fabric of culture in the West, it
is a relatively new development per what we have discussed
earlier. In the Eastern cultures, where historically we can
in only a few exceptional cases observe radical materialism
(which also only remotely resembles the Western version),
the strict division between body and spirit/soul is not found.

If we consider for example the different yoga philosophies
of India, we recognize the common denominator despite a
huge variation in the details, namely that a causal relationship

can always be observed between the mental and the physical processes. It is therefore a typical Western misreading of the facts to speak of pure "body yoga," as if yoga would ever restrict itself to the purely corporeal. (As a consequence, the yoga offered as training in Western fitness centers has only little in common with the original yoga from India.) Nevertheless, in the various schools and philosophical systems are certain specializations for the physical part of it such as Hatha yoga. Yet even the most single-minded of Hatha yogis would never presume to claim that they were only doing it for the *physical* effects or that these might also be only conceptually separable in a clear way from spiritual-psychological processes and states. In other words: The different yoga schools might well distribute their priorities differently between the physical and the spiritual, but on a basic level they never question the unity of both.

Chinese philosophy proceeds in much the same way, in that it observes a close connection between physical condition and moral and ethical behavior. It considers for instance in the concept of subtle chi as not simply some kind of "energy" of objectifiable nature neutral in value as electricity is for example in Western thinking. In contrast with the way it is often dealt with in Western fitness and martial arts studios, you can't arrive at a mastery and deployment of chi according to Chinese holistic modalities merely through the mastery of certain forms of bodily gymnastics, just as Indian prana (life energy) gets exhaustively described as "subtle" and as a physical power "which is simply not *yet* detectable using today's instruments." The same goes for Polynesian *Manas* as well as for countless other energy concepts from older world cultures.

Again in the nineteenth century people in the realm of Western culture used to speak quite freely of "vital energy" which was called *vril* (possibly derived from the Latin *vis*, "power, energy," in conjunction with *virilitas*, "virility, manliness") by the English novelist and Rosicrucian Edward Bulwer-Lytton, and even several decades before him as *od* (derived from *odin*) by the German metallurgist, naturalist, and discoverer of paraffin, Karl von Reichenbach. If we really wanted to investigate the issue in detail, it would go beyond the scope of this book, but we should at least permit ourselves the observation that it was rather more likely the inadequate scientific knowledge of later esoteric authors that led to these concepts being sweepingly and simplistically equated with "a kind of electricity."

Chinese *chi* (also: qi, qì, ch'i, ki, gi) has become well-known in the West. As the traditional teachings of ancient China were largely frowned upon during Mao's regime, there are still even today a whole series of crudely materialistic explanatory approaches out there still, with the help of which Chinese researchers—above all physicians, but physiologists and martial artists too—compare chi to what even today is called "subtle energy" in Western esotericism. While this is not fundamentally wrong from a traditional perspective, it is very one-sided and limited. It is more appropriate to define chi as "potential": a perspective not limited to the energetic, but which also covers structural and primarily procedural aspects of the human body, its motor skills and its organized actions. As the well-founded practice of acupuncture—which builds in a quite fundamental way upon the concept of chi—continually shows, it is less about which ways and forms, aggregate conditions and intensities, this "energy" assumes, than about the *overall organization* of the human being, which is not in turn restricted only to the body. In other words: If we take the example of the Chinese martial arts, particularly the so-called inner style, what is most important is not merely the intention to activate chi, to bundle it up, to compress or steer it somewhere else in order to bring about a physical effect such as contactless pushing or repelling attackers and the like. To do this actually requires rather more of an overall sense of organization and method of fine control for which the term "chi" is really only an overarching metaphor.

Ultimately, the existence of neither chi, nor animal magnetism, vril, od, or manas, can be proven beyond doubt by today's scientific standards and the currently available technological means. Right now, we don't need to concern ourselves with it any further because really, the possibility theoretically exists that this verification might happen at a later point in time when we have at our disposal better measuring instruments and techniques, a situation that has indeed been the case throughout science's history. Such an energy concept would then still be very useful, at least as a working hypothesis. In actuality, today it is already proving itself to be utterly superfluous. Therefore, sticking with the example of martial arts, it is demonstrably perfectly possible to dispense entirely with the postulate of chi or any other "subtle energy" and still generate the physical effects associated with it both in oneself and also in an opponent. Consequently, there is a whole series of admittedly more "modern" than traditionally oriented martial arts trends that don't waste any time on a definition (not to mention any practical inclusion) of chi or similarly speculative forms of energy.

We will also do the same here in the course of our training. You are at liberty to continue to engage with chi or "subtle energies" and even to "believe" in them. If you don't consider this right or even merely useful, you'll find nothing on the following pages to alter your course. But if you are not familiar with the concept of chi or still not convinced of it, you need not feel that we are preventing you from integrating the methods presented here into your everyday practice.

Of essential significance is above all the recognition that a whole lot more resides behind the term "body" than the outward biological form or physique. The differentiation we retain here between *body, mind,* and *soul* in this case has merely a didactic purpose. It describes a method of mediation and does not purport to enforce a strict and definitive division between the three fields. In that regard, we are working here with a conscious blurring; this segmentation is in no way all that accurately definable in practice. Here as well it's ultimately all about a *holistic* outlook and treatment. And this is not diminished in any way by the three postulated segments. Because the fictitious dividing line between theory and practice also dissolves in actual application and implementation.

Mind

In the following pages we understand "mind" to be that which is commonly referred to as intellect, cognition, consciousness, perception, observation, and decision-making abilities or basic cognition. We see, by means of this variety of terms, which has evolved historically for the most part, that with the *mind* in a quite similar way as with the *body* we are talking about a very complex concept or phenomenon. Here we would also do well to be aware of the various aspects and ways of seeing connected with this designation. Even if initially it might seem somewhat confusing, this ultimately facilitates a differentiating and efficient approach that is simply superior to a heavy-handed reductionist consideration in the sense that mind = intellect.

As the previously mentioned Anton Mesmer made it explicit on a grand scale in his own time, the fact that what is mental, as with what is spiritual, can exert a massive and even spectacular influence on the physical (contrary to what was believed for a long time) was not without its consequences.

In the long run, it provided for a few surprises and alterations to the Western image of humanity. It's certainly true that there was nothing like such a strict separation made between body and mind in the everyday practices of ancient Greece as we can read it in the works of Greek philosophy that still dominate aspects of world knowledge. In medieval scholasticism as well, sometimes very sophisticated observations can be found upon the actual (therefore not purely theoretical and abstract) relationship between body, mind, and soul. It is also undeniable that more than anything, it was Christian teachings on salvation in their estimation that bestowed a subordinate or even blatantly demoted role upon both the body and the mind. Its only concern was—as it was in the religion of ancient Egypt—to reclaim for itself and thus safeguard life in the hereafter, meaning after physical death, so the ascended soul would partake in eternal bliss and simultaneously escape from the danger of damnation. The process was imagined to be final and eternal, rendering the body as the soul's "prison." Likewise, the mind was understood as an exclusively corporeal and ephemeral function without any value in the hereafter.

In a somewhat shortened historical overview, it is thanks to the Age of Enlightenment that the primacy of the physical and the mental in the world was set in opposition against a sole fixation on afterlife salvation. A lot of ink has already flowed on the extent to which "Project Enlightenment" has come to an end, failed, or is perhaps only just in its infancy.

We cannot and will not delve any deeper here into the subject. We only felt that we needed to point it out here in order to make it clear that the validity of concentrating merely on the physical is in no way as obvious and indisputable as, for example, the representatives of a rationalistic science and philosophy often depict it to be *or* as we know it from our lives as they are experienced today. In this respect it falls to us (under circumstances that are not always easy for us personally) to deal with this subject with a levelheaded openness regarding the outcome.

Even the philosophers, political and social theorists, and educators of the Enlightenment were and still remained predominately tied to the Christian understanding of the primacy of the spiritual. This meant that they would only be able to revolt and not actually have the means to argue against a metaphysical position which was improvable or considered irrelevant in dealing with the world as might have been put forward in a vehement fashion by the clergy of the established religions or by the social classes bound closely to them (the royal court, the aristocracy, the administrative classes, and so on). It would actually last a good two hundred years longer, until utilitarianism and pragmatism would form an alliance with secularism, materialism, and positivism. What is commonly termed "rationalism" or "skepticism" dates back mainly to this union. At least in the Western cultural domain, the world view of the natural sciences and the prevailing political and social theories are today almost exclusively shaped by these ideological elements. The separation between religion and politics, church and state, self-evident to the democratic understanding in the West today and remaining profoundly alien to the cultures and ideologies primarily influenced by Islam (as an example) is an offshoot of this development.

Today we consider religion for all intents a private matter, a concept actually first formulated in Europe with the Peace of Westphalia, which put to a permanent end the religiously motivated armed combats in Europe. The basis for this change in perspective was of course that religious belief could not be objectified. Once past a certain level of development in technological, scientific, and economic prosperity, it could no longer serve as a reliable starting point for a community that was looking to evolve further still. Now more flexibility was required in all spheres to include a society's worldview, religion, and social ethics. However, this has brought about no cessation in the religious arguments between the representatives of the various confessions and denominations; rather, with this, religion and metaphysics took on the character instead of an absolutely binding overall social foundation for all parties, at least in the Western understanding of the world. This development still seems to continue coming to the fore even more than it did despite all religious-sectarian revival efforts and counter-agitations.

In theology and metaphysics, mind comes close to spirit and will often in turn be equated or even merged with the concept of a soul. We arrive thus at a blurring of our terms, something one could safely describe as hopeless shambles when expressed much less subtly. Something that also proves to be just as unhelpful in this matter is the fact that "spirit" is often treated as synonymous with "ghost" and what's more, not just the phantasm of a wandering dead person but with the undead, the revenants, and invisible presences of all kinds. As a result, the term "spirit" is still often equated with a nonmaterial or subtle essence; the spectrum ranges from "good" helpful spirits to "evil" demons but does not really contribute to a clarification of our terms.

Here we are using this triple structure of body–mind/spirit–soul primarily for didactic purposes so that we don't have to continue struggling with this cultural/historical ballast. If you are interested in further reading, you are well advised to keep these pointers at hand mentally, so you can assign the use of the term "mind" correspondingly with other authors. Doing so helps avoid confusion and ensures that you can draw more benefit from this reading without any additional effort.

The term "mind" will be used in this book exclusively to describe cognition, understanding, reason, consciousness, and thinking activity. We will also treat the concept of mind as the perception and implementation of whatever our senses deliver to us in conscious impressions and information. And once again: this is just for didactic/pedagogical reasons. It facilitates the mediation of approaches and processes, but we won't create any dogma regarding the mind's isolated self-sufficiency. So this book won't claim that mind exists as it were in a vacuum, independent of the body and soul. The exact opposite is the case, of course! And if we point out here once again that in the practice of implementation it's always a matter of taking a *holistic* approach, then this is done for a good reason and will also be brought up once more later on.

Human comprehension tends to segment the perceived world in an enthusiastic fashion and to consider the resultant fragments in isolation such that they are completely independent of each other. Culture and civilization are based precisely upon manufacturing and maintaining a collective consensus over which categories, schemata, basic structures, or drawers (for a more casual expression) into which the world might be divided. For millennia, the spiritual traditions of countless cultures have continually revolted against this holier-than-thou classifying. No matter if these approaches were (or still are) successful or doomed to failure, they also make clear that we, in every attempt to control our surroundings, our social environment, and ourselves, must never lose sight of the fact that we are always tasked to deal with the whole and not just trite extracts or partial aspects.

It is indeed easy to expect others to engage with the world holistically. It is readily apparent as well, though, how difficult it can actually be as soon as we try to do it ourselves. Reason, cognition, thinking—they all segment or even atomize the world. They break it down into seemingly isolated structures and processes that can be controlled more easily (albeit merely on a superficial level) than that big picture in the face of which the "little" individual would be hopelessly overwhelmed. Thus runs the argument as it is reflected in numerous variations in current scientific methodology, philosophy, and cognitive research. There are, however, a host of technical, well-justified reasons to carry on this way, at least for a limited period. Closer observation of strictly isolated single extracts can definitely help us towards some knowledge of the bigger picture. And since this is the way the human mind operates and can on the face of it only truly soar by employing the way of segmentation and contouring (meaning via the marginalization of the whole into useful pieces of knowledge), we should also motivate ourselves to become even-handed when approaching this fragmented constitution and to take it as far as it could go after it runs out of steam of its own accord. That's not to say that we should stop there, however.

For the purposes of our discussions, we will always return to conventional findings and recommendations from depth psychology, neuropsychology, brain research, and the social sciences within these pages. You are free to implement these approaches and recommendations as procedural instructions, modify them, or discard them. Please note, however, that we are always employing a holistic approach despite the previously mentioned body-mind-soul division. To this extent, the recommendations for the physical, the mental, and the spiritual are harmonized with each other and should always also be implemented with that in mind.

Soul

If the category "mind" is already influenced by a multitude of different definitions and contradictory points of view mostly historically and culturally conditioned, we find this is so much more the case with the term "soul." We determined in the previous section that the soul is often equated with the mind/spirit and is defined in a confusingly similar way.

Of course there are also other approaches, like for example theology and metaphysics. There, the soul is usually understood as a separate entity depending upon the particular religion or ideological tradition. This detached entity "inhabits" the body, albeit on a temporary basis, and according to some belief systems it is even held hostage there. Such ways of thinking and believing always develop a hierarchy in which the soul is regarded as the most important principle availing itself of the body and its tools, meaning the limbs and organs, and the collective senses, but also the mind and its thought processes. At least in this way the soul remains exempt from the body/mind setup. The claim arises here out of the postulation that the soul qualifies for a form of immortality or at least that it can survive death regardless of whether it returns to the material world afterward through rebirth ("reincarnation" does literally mean "becoming flesh again") or whether it enters a new otherworldly environment that might be called the underworld, Hades, heaven, purgatory, hell, and so on. As it has been stated on many occasions: most of us believe that we consist of an animal body that harbors an angel's soul. The stages of life are prioritized along these lines as well. The earthbound life takes on the character of a stopover, a halfway house, or a probationary period. In any case, the emphasis is still placed upon the "real" life, after death.

The most influential historical expression by far of this concept of the soul in our cultural sphere was found in ancient Egypt. Here the soul and afterlife beliefs of the three great monotheistic religions—Judaism, Christianity, and Islam—have their origin. Even the fundamental concept of monotheism (that an almighty and all-knowing God created the world and rules over it alone) can already be found prefigured in the admittedly short-lived but very influential heresy of the pharaoh Akhenaten (Amenhotep IV), who tried to assert his Aten or solar disc cult over the traditional polytheism of Egyptian religion.

The culture of the ancient Egyptians overall was very life-affirming and positive about the world; the joyless body hostility of later Christianity was completely foreign to them. That said, Egypt's unbroken, five thousand year-old culture naturally went through many very different ideological phases, so we should be careful to not make excessively broad generalizations. After all that we have learnt about Egyptian religion and its verifiable expression through culture, be it in the field of city planning and architecture or with respect to its religious art and burial rites, it placed the focus of its interest on life in the hereafter like no other ever has. The practice went so far that those who could at least afford it would invest considerably more of their resources in the construction and design of their tombs and memorials than in their current earthly dwellings. The commonly used phrase "marble for the mausoleum, mud huts for everyday life" may be somewhat exaggerated, but it describes reasonably accurately the actual situation. The sheer number of Egyptian mummies—estimated to run to several hundred million, of which admittedly only a fraction have been excavated so far—makes it unquestionably clear how important the survival of the soul in the *Amenti*, the underworld, was to them. In this afterlife and through the tests the soul had endure there, the center of the matter was always about eternity and thus about an imperishable existence (as opposed to ephemeral earthly life). It stood at the true midpoint of all ancient Egyptian culture.

This cultural emphasis is not some abstract cultural phenomenon. Rather it touches upon Egypt's existential self-understanding accustomed to this soul paradigm in every aspect of life and therefore in everything most fundamental. So it is no exaggeration to claim that our outlook even today on humanity and life is still strongly linked to it, at least insofar as the monotheistic descendants of ancient Egyptian religion still affect it.

There was also an awareness of the soul in Hellenistic antiquity that developed in part a quite sophisticated concept of life in the beyond after death. As in Egypt, the prospect of reward and punishment in life after death formed the basis for the morals and ethics of the time.

Whoever transgressed against religious, moral, or ethical standards in his or her earthly life had to reckon with and account for their soul in the hereafter. In the underworld, the soul went through rigorous tests in which abstinence from sin, the pursuit of truthfulness and therefore a morally impeccable existence were expected. For this was a precondition for the soul on its journey through the afterlife not to be given over to the devastating forces that held sway in the underworld. So in peoples' everyday lives of those times, pressure was exerted on believers to apply an ethical mode of conduct to their physical life so they wouldn't forfeit eternal bliss in the hereafter. Less formal and ritually constructed than the Egyptian *Amenti* are the Elysian Fields of the Greek Hades which were reserved for those souls who had accomplished greatness and morally laudable deeds in this world. Everyone else was damned to cross over eventually into nonexistence. In this respect, it is worth noting that early Judaism, developed out of the twelve tribal religions of the later people of Israel into the first monotheistic world religion, placed no great emphasis upon life in the hereafter. These sorts of ideas didn't initially arise until much later on, and what's more, didn't ever assume a dominant position within the Jewish religious character. Even today the religion of Moses is rather vague in its pronouncements about the afterlife. Its prime focus is unmistakably upon the observance of the divine laws in everyday life in this existence.

Because Roman culture was pragmatic in this regard, they largely adopted the mythology and the pantheon of ancient Greece and adapted them according to their own moral values. In terms of interesting characteristic developments, we should make particular mention in this context of the mystery cults, then in great vogue during the later Roman Empire. They were to a great extent influenced by Hellenistic and Anatolian beliefs but above all by the cult forms of Egypt. If we generalize, we can say that a gradual development upward and a purification of the soul were promised to the adepts of the mystery cults. These adepts were sorted into hierarchically graded degrees of initiation based on cultic and ritualistic actions. Here the mystic went through a regulated purification process that not only helped his or her soul to a further edification in this world as well as in the other but also aimed as well to ensure a participation in divine immortality. The parallels with later (particularly medieval) Christian mysticism can be seen clearly. Hermetic spirituality, by contrast, is undergoing ever more new manifestations even today yet is also characterized by this basic idea.

Early Christianity first achieved prominence as a sect within the Jewish community of faiths but soon broke free from the Jewish religion of law. It then set itself up as the fulfillment of what the Mosianic faith had always promised: Jesus of Nazareth is understood as the promised Messiah in Christianity as well as for Jewish Christians today.

This book is not the place to follow up on detailed theologic-historical developments. Nevertheless, we should make the point that according to the current state of research, Christianity as we know it today actually crystallized out of a variety of Gnostic schools of life and religious communities. It might also explain how we managed to arrive at the overly strong emphasis on the soul, so characteristic of Christianity. Here again for reasons of space we can unfortunately only make broad generalizations. Put briefly, most Gnostic schools see this material world as the wicked creation of a subordinate Godhead understood to be limited for the most part to actions that are stupid and also partly evil, having nothing to do with the "True God" and who in some cases gets mistaken for Him. This "pseudo God," usually called the demiurge, is equated with the Jehovah of the Old Testament (the Tetragrammaton—"the one of four letters," which in Hebrew is Y-H-V-H). With regard to what we are examining, it is significant that the schools of life and cults generally classified together under the term "gnosis" or "gnosticism" make the assumption that a "divine spark" is peculiar to humanity (or according to some opinions, all living things), which is itself consubstantial to the original and good God. It is the job of these divine sparks after physical death, to maneuver their way back into the realm of the Pleroma ("fullness") by circumventing the ignorant/evil demiurge ("the builder") or "false God" and his henchmen called the archons. The otherworldly life after death is thus also declared here to be the main goal of existence. However as a general rule, the Gnostics were unaware of both the concept of sin and the later principle of collective Original Sin, propagated even today by Christianity, from which the Nazarene was supposed to have redeemed humanity through his death on the cross.

The Gnostic cults and the established Christianity of Saint Paul stood in sharp competition with each other. This rivalry ended with the victory of early-established Christianity, but it was a long road to get to this point, spanning almost four centuries, characterized by dogmatic conflicts and upheavals. For the development of the concept of the soul, as it is familiar to us today through the victorious "official" Christianity, it was crucial that the Gnostic conception of the divine spark (*pneuma* in Greek) mutated into the mainstream Christian definition of the soul, in which a self-sufficient, coherent in itself and above all individual, unique being was identified, whose earthly existence is only a guest appearance, for the duration of which the body, including cognition and perception (that is, the mind) is available to it as a vehicle.

Now in this historical overview we have reached a conception of the soul that has remained largely unchanged in the various Christian denominations until today. The overwhelming power of the Christian church since its elevation to the Roman state religion by Emperor Constantine, but above all in the Middle Ages which followed on from the collapse of the Roman Empire, has ensured that the concept of the soul has become a constant in Western culture, which you could never dismiss, at least not until the Age of Enlightenment dawned. You have to keep in mind that this was not just out of a concern for theology. For our entire Western culture was and is in fact influenced by it in every area of life. Philosophy, morals and ethics, our understanding of law and justice, political theory and burial rites, the science of nutrition, medicine, alchemy, astrology, mysticism, and the teachings on harmonics of pre-scientific natural philosophy—all this is permeated by the Christian primacy of the unique, certainly not all-powerful but, to the individual, all-meaningful for the individual soul. Its well-being and ultimate care are of primary importance for all human endeavors.

Should you be someone who has no interest in religion due to your upbringing as a child or because of a later turning away from religious perspectives on the world, you might perhaps consider it an exaggeration to attach such great importance to the Christian concept of the soul. But don't worry; even if you can't get away from it when you look closely at the history of Western ideas, within the scope of this book it's completely insignificant which religious convictions you have made your own, or have rejected for your own purposes. It's only important to grasp these connections because when dealing with our social environment, they don't just help explain all sorts of specific things but they also offer helpful hints when it comes to ensuring the protection of our own integrity.

Of course the Western understanding of the soul has changed since the Enlightenment not only because the supremacy of the Christian churches has been broken, rendering them unable to act as sole arbiters in determining the way of thinking and the self-image of Western humanity. More generally, the transcendent and the metaphysical, hence also the spiritual and (here it is again!) the soul-based, have been and are increasingly called into question. If psychology since Sigmund Freud has been understood as "the science of the soul," what is actually meant is not knowledge of a transcendent, subtle state of being perhaps associated with an otherworldly realm, but much more a strictly worldly feature we generally refer to as "psyche" or "psychological state" without bringing into play any religious undertones. In non-religious and extra-metaphysical contexts, soul today denotes primarily that which can be summarized under the umbrella term "personality." To this also belongs the life of feelings (if we follow the definition psychology uses) and the ensuing emotional structures, processes, and behavior patterns that determine our earthly existence to a large and even preeminent extent.

Fortunately, we need dwell here no longer on long-winded philosophical/metaphysical or religious niceties. You are at complete liberty to conceive of the soul in the Christian sense or in any other, and alternatively to understand it in a completely ametaphysical way as well, as it is common to do in today's cognitive sciences, psychology, psychiatry, and anthropology. So when we actually use terms here like "self," "I," or "soul" interchangeably, it will be because we are concerned with a holistic and therefore all-embracing approach; the threefold division of body-mind-soul, already mentioned many times, might only be a didactic expedient anyway. In reality, we want to actualize the effective protection of the integral human being in its entirety and thus everything inevitably meshes together. The amalgamation takes into account belief systems, religion, and metaphysics only in as much as these might be of relevance for personal self-understanding.

You will find in the following chapters in the respective sections on "soul" the most diverse set of methods and techniques from across a variety of spiritual traditions. The spectrum ranges from shamanism via Eastern meditation teachings and mysticism, alchemy and magic, to the mystery cults and contemporary consciousness schools. Our approach is completely nondogmatic in the sense that it requires no belief models, doing away with the usual cultural and traditionalist ballast.

As is appropriate for free men and women, it is completely up to you what you might want to believe or not, what moral/ethical standards authoritatively apply to you or what you might for yourself prefer to disregard. In order to obtain the greatest possible benefit from what follows, all you should bring with you are open-mindedness and the readiness to experiment. Much might appear familiar to you; other things may surprise you. Perhaps it will also provoke doubts and questions. This is not only perfectly fine but also thoroughly desirable: only your own questions married with a relentless desire for exploration of the world as open-ended as possible in nature (but still always concerned with efficiency and effectiveness) can truly help you progress. Whoever believes they can always have complete answers to all of life's questions down pat not only makes themselves guilty of megalomania and arrogance but also prevents any chances of further development. Perfection means completeness, a state that does not permit any further improvement—hence it is understood here as a metaphor for death and entropy.

To briefly summarize: What we colloquially designate as soul turns out to be a complex mesh of extremely diverse individual elements (body, mind, psyche) on closer inspection. When it comes to our overriding viewpoint, it's a question of wholeness, of which we can deny no single component without suffering as a result. So the "personality" is also related to the "corporeal"; "thinking" can't really be distinguished from the "motoric"; "perception" causes our "bodily" well-being; we can influence our "disposition" with the aid of an effective physical modulation and vice versa; our social connectivity through family, friends, enemies, colleagues, or passing acquaintances affects our "self-understanding"; and much more. Soul protection, which to all practical purposes is the central focus of this work, means taking seriously one's own integrity and therefore wholeness as well as realizing one's self-assertiveness above and beyond mere ego-reinforcement in the world as well as in one's own social surroundings. The reason? The ego is always getting confused with individuality or even with individuation, as postulated by C. G. Jung. We will deal more fully with these issues in the next chapter. It should suffice to say that you are far more than the feeble construct of a "personality," at its core only socially substantiated and thus exposed to challenges, a notion contemporary psychology and the philosophy of cognition would say is your due. Soul means here the totality that is substantially more than the sum of its parts, a dynamic network of different compositions that might need extra molding and stabilization but which thereby also receives effective access to the world and the happiness in life which is its due. This book is dedicated to the examination and development of this dynamic.

2

WITHOUT STRESS AND WITHOUT AMBITION

Instruction Manual for Your
Magical Shield Training

First of all: *no stress!* That's easy to say, but when we are first confronted with the frustration of failure, we forget all our good intentions only too quickly. And yet, all the same: *no stress!* (At least when it comes to our magical shield training.) No, not everything must and will be fun. Much will be demanding, at times maybe even very demanding, and none of it lends itself to rapid consumption.

Consider first your age. Whether you are twenty, forty, sixty, or eighty, this is the length of time needed to make yourself into who you are today. Not all of it will have been good and right, not all bad and wrong. If you have gotten this far in reading this book, you are allowed to make the

assumption that there's more to life for you than the maintenance of your personal status quo. In other words: You want
to develop yourself further. What that means exactly, you
alone know. It could be that a vague feeling of inadequacy is
driving you on, a hungry, perhaps even greedy "there must
be more to life" feeling; perhaps it is even resentment about
the injustice in the world, the failure of your efforts to realize
your wishes and desires, and maybe also the acute demands
of an uneasy, oppressive life situation.

Before actively turning your attention to the implementation of our protective shield program (properly taking
shape in the next chapter), first of all you should put together
a catalog of the real and alleged hindrances that have made
the successful attainment of your life goals unrealizable up to
now, and whatever may be doing so still.

These setbacks can be personal shortcomings: "When it
comes to making things, I have two left hands," "In my case,
good taste is pure luck," "I am not very good with languages,"
"I look awful," "I am much too shy," "I am too fat/ugly/too
thin/unattractive," "women/men frighten me," and so on.
It could also be that sudden mental block that precedes
speaking in front of a large group of people, the stomach
cramp of stage fright, being unexpectedly struck dumb where
a friendly word of comfort would have changed everything.
The hindrances are also those beloved fellow human beings
and their not always particularly friendly behavior: the
obnoxious landlord who provoked relentlessly you until you

lashed out—very much to your regret in the subsequent criminal proceedings; the colleague who disparaged you in front of the boss and who got you into trouble with a disciplinary procedure; the scheming snake who snatched away your hoped-for promotion within the company; the best friend suddenly caught in bed with your partner; the drunk who not only smashed your car into scrap metal but also has to answer for half your family; your mother, who was not ashamed to report you to the police; your father, who made you look foolish in front of your first boyfriend; the long-term business partner who suddenly disappeared with the company assets. The setbacks are illnesses, blows of fate, evil and malicious coincidences as well as fears and neuroses, simple mistakes like gross misjudgments, addictions and dependencies, naive behavior, and calculated but failed acts. As comprehensively as you can, list everything that might apply to your life.

Do it in writing. Take time with it, be thorough, and also quietly enjoy the fact that you only need to do all this once! It might take a few days to do it, but take it seriously and don't forget that you can only deceive yourself, no one else. This list is obviously not meant for others, and what's more you will be destroying it again later. Before the destruction, there is yet one more thing to do.

When the written list is finished, satisfy yourself one more time that you really proceeded with it as carefully and as self-critically as you could. No one is demanding you do any more than you can; the only expectation is that you don't do less than whatever is within your capabilities. More won't make a difference anyway. For sure, this is an utter truism we unfortunately all too often overlook in the day-to-day rush. Incidentally, your list doesn't have to be chronological or otherwise sorted in any way. You can simply and without any hesitation add any further points at the end if they occur to you during the review.

Now at last it's time to get started. Make sure you will be completely undisturbed for quite a while. Unplug the phone and switch off your smartphone. Lock yourself in your room or hang a Do Not Disturb sign on the door. Put the list in front of you so you can access it without any difficulty, and have a black marker pen ready.

You definitely don't have to do the list all at once. Depending on how long it's taking, you might possibly need a few extra sessions, and you can spread it gently across several days, according to your needs and the opportunities you get.

Assume a comfortable seating position. If you are an experienced yogi or accomplished yogini, you can choose the Lotus or Half-Lotus, but it is really not essential. The main thing is that you are comfortable and sitting as upright as possible without giving yourself cramps or pain. If you are bedridden or confined to a wheelchair, simply adjust your position accordingly.

Breathe in and out deeply and calmly around ten times. Only then pick up your list and look at the first item on it.

Read what you have written there quietly—in complete calm! —and carefully. Close your eyes and once more literally picture what you have described. Is what you wrote down vividly there in front of your inner eye, or strictly speaking before your inner perception? (It doesn't necessarily have to be perceived in a visual sense.) Don't bother making any internal comment on it, don't assign any resources to regretting your action or pitying yourself. In fact, don't cultivate feelings of remorse or engage with it emotionally in any way whatsoever. Be as impartial an observer as you can be, someone for whom all the events are still registering free of judgment, striving for complete neutrality taking up no position on it.

Let the image or whatever you would like to call this inner perception gently pull away without granting it even the slightest bit of additional attention. That's really not so hard. Human consciousness already has enough bedlam going on inside it, and thoughts constantly wander off all by themselves when you don't expressly force them to stay in line. But please don't get confused: don't just distract yourself until the item on your list has cleared from your consciousness; merely give it the opportunity to fade away on its own and disappear out of your consciousness.

Once this is done, open your eyes again, take the black marker you have at the ready, and strike the item you have dealt with from your list. Make sure that it's completely illegible. As we have said already, you will only use this list one time. In symbolic terms you have now erased the first negative point from your life balance.

Again so there is no confusion: No one is claiming that by doing this your problem has already dissolved into thin air. This is neither the point of this process, nor should you maintain any hopes along these lines be it secretly or openly. Instead you have now kick-started a healing and corrective process that will make you immune against later harm, even if that harm might be of a completely different nature. Neither should you entertain secret hopes of any kind of spectacular sudden "augmented brain waves," "insights," or anything like that either. This is not what this is all about.

It bears repeating: Serenity is the key!

Once you have fully processed and symbolically neutralized these "negative life reflections" (but really only then!), you should apply yourself to the "basic training" in the next chapter. It lays the foundations for everything, which is dealt with and recommended in the following chapters.

You will notice that in the chapters to come we will follow the tripartite structure of body-mind-soul, which we have already discussed extensively, and that there are discussions and instructions corresponding to each of these segments. These are self-explanatory and require no further elucidation here. However, there is yet a fourth element that's added, namely the "protocols." There are at any given time four protocols per chapter, and if you work on one of these per week, you have approximately one month to work through them. This suggestion is based upon the consideration that the working through of these separate protocols also requires a lot of following up—whether it's because it throws up issues you would like to go back over, or even that it sets off mental and emotional processes that you would like to subject to closer inspection.

The protocols consist of separate phases, which will in each case be described and then explained in a concise way. This can range from a period of purely lying down without any further requirements, with the exception of staying awake with the least possible outward movement (other than breathing), right up to complex mudras, spatial movements, and the like. The description of each phase is always situated underneath the relevant protocol plan, so in precisely the position where the content of the individual phase is repeated. This saves you the time-consuming looking and matching up, and you'll be grateful for this with the increasing number of protocols you have to complete.

It may be that the description of one or other of the phases seems to be too concise or even difficult to understand. This is not the express intention, and it is not deliberately formulated to be convoluted or difficult to fathom. On the other hand, the description does also correspond explicitly to the procedure. Do just what you are able to do with these instructions! Don't worry about any possible "misunderstandings" or even about whether you might have done something "wrong." In this regard there is *no* right or wrong, as long as you maintain the serious effort to carry it out as well and as carefully as you can, according to your current understanding and your abilities. We have already intimated this and we underline it here one more time: It's not a question of doing "more" than you can; it's much more about *not doing less* than you are capable of. In this way you will spare yourself from the ultimately always self-destructive, and at its core unrealistic, demand that you should strive beyond your existing capabilities. That is not just impossible, but it also leads to an overload, to a hope-less (in the truest sense of the word) overburdening and ultimately to self-inflicted failure.

There is a reason why the term used here is *protocols* and not *exercises*. Exercises commonly mean procedures that place failure in the foreground from the outset. If an exercise succeeds straight away, ultimately it won't have had any reason for existing in the first place! Exercises are based on the assumption that the command of a process can be achieved through repetition of failure, whether it be learning a foreign language, the mastering of a physical (maybe athletic) performance or the development of a particular required sensitivity. Thus exercises always demand to be repeated, and this is precisely not the case with the protocols. Instead the following applies: each protocol only actually needs to be performed once in a lifetime.

This might have both a reassuring and a terrifying effect at the same time. The realization that the protocols are anything but unassuming and that they need to be implemented in regulation time is certainly reassuring. The "fun factor" does not play an express role in it but does not permit the opposite conclusion either, i.e., that it's all about a loftier form of self-torture.

These protocols might therefore be thoroughly challenging and sometimes maybe exhausting to implement as well. But—this is where the terrifying aspect might reside—the fact that you will only have one single occasion on which to do it also means of course that you only have one single chance to engage exhaustively with the respective protocol. Obviously no one can prevent you from getting attached to the ongoing achievement and success delusion by working through a protocol once again, when for some reason or other you might have had to break it off. However, consider yourself now to have been urgently dissuaded from this! Treat these protocols much more as what they are, *one-off opportunities* to undergo accurately measured and precisely defined processes in the course of this training to overcome them.

To stay with our example: If you must break off one of these protocols for whatever reason and can't see it through to the end, this then is just the end result of your approach to it. Take it seriously, reflect on it, as far as there is anything to reflect on, but resist the temptation to demand a second chance. If you were to stumble into a combat situation of a physical, intellectual, or psychological nature in your everyday life, for example, you wouldn't give your opponent any second chances either.

As a rule, a person will avoid an obligation like the devil avoids the proverbial holy water. This also does not contradict the fact that he or she likes to claim every supposedly absolute truth for themselves. When faced with absolutes, they can exquisitely deny their own responsibility and thus surrender the field to non-commitment. An excellent example of this is the genius cult of the nineteenth century. In as much as artists, poets, thinkers, and scientists were feted for having a particular talent or even genius, one could set one's self up comfortably in mediocrity. If I have no talent, then I don't need to give myself any trouble, do I? In our current context, commitment means not in the least looking at our own failures and the times we fall short (here in the sense of the non-fulfillment of a self-imposed achievement curriculum) soberly without glossing over or downplaying anything—but even more than that... and this really can't be emphasized often enough—*without clinging on or emotionally attaching to it.*

The Buddhist principle of mindfulness and the Yogic injunction to non-attachment reach their culmination in the formulation of the English artist and mage Austin Osman Spare (1886–1956), who compressed them as well as anyone into his formula of non-attachment/non-disinterest. We recommend this attitude to you as well, whenever in the course of this training (and of course on other occasions!) you are occupied with the protection of your own integrity. Disinterest alone would not be enough, which is why Spare also expressly precluded it. On the other hand, attachment means nothing more than dependency and therefore vulnerability—again, nothing that would serve to protect you.

Protocols

The question regarding the importance of the protocols recommended here remains, and what follows really can't be emphasized enough. Even if in your opinion on superficial consideration they don't at first seem to have any apparent connection with the main theme in their corresponding chapters, carry them out as carefully as you can and with optimal diligence. All of them have been tested in practice and have already helped many people establish, expand, and consolidate their own integrity. They are ends in themselves in so far as they simultaneously concretize and define the process of empowerment being presented. They also give sufficient but clearly defined space to the inevitable failures and shortcomings (after all, it is innate to human beings as it is to a thoroughly unconscious animal). The fact that they are presented here as unique and unrepeatable opportunities for you to engage with the various forms of articulation of your body, your mind and your soul, without losing yourself in any postulated causality curve, makes these protocols what they aim to be: the basis and continuation for your integrity as a human *and* a spiritual being.

GENERAL TECHNICAL
INSTRUCTIONS FOR THE PROTOCOLS
Your Timing

The schedules, presented in relation to the individual protocols, are merely to be understood as models. Therefore, they are intended as reference time periods. The exact hours of the day can and should be individually customized (for carrying out the protocol in the late morning, in the afternoon, etc.). In performing them, however, the lengths themselves of the individual phases are binding and must be strictly observed.

On the Report

Report: The Report is carried out immediately straight after the end of the complete set of protocols following a short break of up to five minutes maximum that can be used for activities like going to the bathroom, stretching arms and legs, and so on. Everything must be written down; the time is divided into two parts.

1. The *Factual Report:* Here you make a list of all the events and of your observations in order to hold on to them. This can be done in the form of keywords, simple sketches, etc. The Factual Report should always be carried out as comprehensively as possible.

2. The *Continuation of the Report:* Here thoughts, ideas, associations, detailed graphic sketches, questions, etc., are examined and clarified with the aim of arriving at worthwhile conclusions and outcomes as well as questions that will lead you further.

3

BASIC TRAINING

Introduction to the Fundamentals

When it comes to the protection of your own self, this straight away raises the legitimate question of who "your self" actually is. This is in no way as trivial as one might initially think. After all, the admonitory inscription "Know Thyself" was long ago adorning the ancient Greek Oracle at Delphi.

Of course, contemporary brain research and neuropsychology make it fairly easy for us to scrutinize critically the concept of an individual self, which was previously considered to be self-evident. Even if we don't want to dwell on ontological hair-splitting, we should always remain aware of the fact that the qualities of the so-called self are anything but self-evident. The ancient questions are modern as well: "Who am I?" "Where do I come from?" "Where am I going?" And of course, they can only be answered on an individual basis. Therefore, we hereby renounce explicitly any claim to do this for you and will use the term self in the following pages only as a designation for the totality of your personality and existence.

If we're talking about basic training, it's important right from the beginning to dispel a possible misunderstanding. In everyday speech, *training* usually refers to a set of designated rules and the frequent repetition of discrete exercises. That is not the case here. What we mean instead by training is an exhaustive and as long-lasting as possible engagement with questioning, discoveries, and experiments; its aim is to enable you to get a handle on yourself and your environment and to broaden and strengthen it. It is also not a question of repeatedly implementing certain techniques and converting them into a rigid exercise program that will continually repeat itself. Aside from this, the mere concept of "repetition" is on closer inspection untenable. Heraclitus knew this already when he said that we can never immerse ourselves into the same river twice. Repetition is at the very least postulated upon the stability of the conditions ahead, and that has never really existed. Not only that, but during the repeated reuptake of a practice, the passage of time has flowed on, and all the other factors and environmental conditions you could conceive of have changed, from air pressure to the temperature and on to your blood cell count, your hormone levels, not to mention the aging process to which we are all subject.

All this means that you don't need to repeat anything; every implementation of what is said here is a new and unprecedented approach, something you could also call an experiment. It's all about open-minded exploration, not the mastery of predetermined levels of development and accomplishment that are determined externally. All the stresses the pursuit of success and inevitable chance of failure install in advance drop away.

Sure, you might not be successful right away with some of what is described and promised here within the basic sense of the guidelines. You might notice, upon more sober reflection, that failure is by no means the exception but rather the rule and the norm both as you experience things personally and as they relate to human activity in general. Perhaps failure's prominent featuring will cast doubt upon some of your habits, for example, always striving for tangible, quantifiable results whenever you set about something. In fact, when it comes to striving for success, failure is already in place at the moment of articulation. (Ultimately to strive for success by necessity makes a reality of the existence and possibility of failure.)

For this very reason Eastern spiritual teachers underlined above all else the precept of non-attachment. In Chinese Taoism is the principle of *wu wei*, commonly rendered as "effortless doing," a state of mind in which we do not cling to an outcome, even if an outcome was in fact intended. It is also the case in Indian karma yoga that you don't grasp for the "fruits of your actions" but rather act as if they are completely insignificant in the actual doing. To clarify, I certainly don't imply any doing "as-if." This mental attitude actually has to be established with the utmost rigor without leaving anything behind when it comes to your original objective, wishes, or desires. This might be more easily said than done, but it does lie well within the bounds of possibility and requires simple mindful persistence to implement it.

Incidentally, this method is not entirely foreign to us. If you are learning a foreign language, exhaustively involved in music, or maybe painting, the fine feeling for nuances of language, sound, or color will only emerge after a while, and what's more, in a different way in every person. A course of pure vocabulary cramming is not enough when learning a language. Stylistic niceties and idiomatic expression are only nurtured through extensive practice whether by reading or tenacious conversational practice on a daily basis. Although musical notation, scales, and harmonic theory might be the basis for a further understanding of all things musical, you will have to train your ear as well, or as the neurologist might say, develop connections between the relevant synapses in your brain until you have also built up a feel for harmony and rhythm. Likewise, in painting lessons you can learn about pencil tips and holding a paintbrush, the principle of the golden ratio as well as the manual mixing of colors or the production of an overall sense of perspective through lines of alignment or shading. Ultimately though, painting is more than the accumulation of manual techniques and is only mastered through continual effort and ongoing preoccupation with the stuff of substance, character, and meaningfulness.

So here's one single slogan to help you further along your way: *Let it grow in you!*

Body: Your Body, That Strange Animal— and How You Can Get to Know It Better

It is certainly not preposterous to suggest that our knowledge today about the human body and its workings stands at a comparatively high level, higher at least than has generally been the case historically. Anatomy, human biology, medicine, toxicology, and social sciences have, just like psychiatry and psychology, contributed to our removal of that mysterious element from the physical vehicle. When Mesmer captivated the salons of Europe shortly before the French Revolution with his animal magnetism and his hypnosis techniques, his true innovation consisted of making it clear to his contemporaries how much influence the mind could have over the corporeal, as we have already noted. It wasn't that the minds of the time hadn't already helped develop a pretty broadly evolved medical system. As a matter of fact, Mesmer continually found himself confronted with resistance from the leading representatives of medicine in his day who took offense at his demonstrations and theatrical promises—and not always without cause. It was also the case that some time had to pass still before hygiene and pharmacology were far enough advanced to reduce the almost unbelievably high infant mortality rate of Mesmer's time, in such a way that collective life expectancy has increased steadily right up until today. Granted, conventional or automated medicine does undoubtedly have its limits, and there are a great number of outstanding reasons for taking alternative healing methods and treatment techniques and their claims for proven success seriously. On the other hand, the successes of conventional medicine are hard to deny.

Strangely, most people consider their own bodies a mystery. We only manage to find out what we can about them with the help of technical instruments and complicated measuring techniques that are anything but intuitive. Can anyone provide details of the composition of their own blood without in-depth laboratory analysis? When was the last time you saw your gall bladder? The lobes of your lungs? Your brain mass? As ridiculous as these questions might sound, they make it clear that the greater part of our physical totality eludes any sensory perception. And even when we seek the assistance of complex technical measuring devices and fluoroscopic apparati, the results remain for the most part completely incomprehensible to us because a relevant amount of study with extensive and on-going professional experience are required for their correct interpretation. And unfortunately even then you are not completely home and dry—there is hardly a radiologist to be found who has a good word for their colleagues' findings or interpretation! It's pretty much the same case with ultrasound images. Although misdiagnoses and an incorrect medical approach are happily not the rule, unfortunately though they are also far from rare. It certainly cannot be denied that despite all the spectacular advances in medical research—especially for medical lay people—the bottom line is that we still know very little about the body and find most of it out through hearsay.

Indeed every reasonable person knows that we need our bodies for everything that we categorize as life on earth. Without a functioning brain, there is no thinking, comprehension, and interpretation of our environment, no communication with others, etc. Whoever cannot walk needs crutches or a wheelchair to compensate for this physical deficiency, otherwise movement remains denied to them. Hunger, thirst, and sleep deprivation, all three of which are also widely used torture techniques, will sooner or later come crashing down upon our peace of mind. And long before they have a life-threatening effect on our organisms, they can drive us downright insane. Ultimately, we need our eyes and ears, our sense of touch and of smell and of course our taste buds also, to be able to really comprehend the world at all on the sensory level.

Within the sphere of this basic training we want to deal primarily (in terms of the technical aspects of the body) with the motoric; that is, bodily movement—walking and running, swinging the arms, and also grasping with fingers, and eyelids shutting. There is also an internal motoric we are at best partially aware of, like our heartbeat, the contractions of our veins and arteries, blood circulation, the workings of our organs like the kidneys and our liver, spleen, and gall bladder, and much more. There is also the external motoric that similarly usually runs more or less unconsciously and thus unnoticed. Examples include breathing, the aforementioned shutting of the eyelids, hair standing on end, or eye movement.

We can continue this list even further. The interplay of our muscles, the tendons shortening and elongating, slight displacements in the tissue, the gas exchange in the cells of our bodies, the growth of our hair and nails, the dying and the regular turnover in our skin cells—these are just a few more examples that could be added to the list. As long as we live, our bodies are both internally and externally constantly in motion, even during the so-called resting state, when breathing, the circulation of the blood, and the beating of the heart are never put on hold. And let's not forget the overall metabolic process, digestion, peristalsis, and so on.

The "resting state" means nothing! On closer examination, it does not exist either in the human body or anywhere at all in the universe. Even mountains and whole landmasses are constantly in motion, no matter that it is barely perceptible to the untrained eye. The earth turns at breakneck speed upon its own axis; planets, solar systems, and galaxies are in pursuit across the universe, which itself is likewise steadily expanding. Good old Heraclitus with his "everything is in flux" knew very well of what he spoke. In the present context, this is of great importance because it leads us towards a means of approach that is indispensable both for one's own magical protection and indeed for protection in a general sense. Everything is in motion and there is no standing still. And, correspondingly, it is also counterproductive to strive for any such thing.

At first, this idea might seem nonsensical to you. In the course of the protocols presented here with their extended periods of lying down in which you should simply lie comfortably but aside from your breathing be outwardly immobile, you will soon notice that even your supposedly motionless body is subject to a vast number of movements. Or maybe you think that you could stand upright for just one second, without moving at all? You can put this quickly to the test: Grab a camera and a tripod, get the right lighting, and film yourself while you try to stand *completely still* in one spot. Watch closely the recording right afterwards. (A tip: Stand in front of a contrasting background, maybe in black clothing against a white wall, which will also make the slightest movement clearly visible.)

The next time you are told by a yoga teacher or martial arts instructor that you have to sit or stand "absolutely still," you'll know exactly what to make of such statements—absolutely nothing!

It's very much the same with human sleep. Some people believe they don't move at all while they are sleeping or only very slightly. Sleep research, however, proved some time ago that this was not the case. Depending on the measuring technique, we make hundreds, perhaps even thousands of large and small movements while we are asleep. Aleister Crowley was fond of joking that you could catapult an elephant into the stratosphere with the energy that an adult human being expends in one night moving while asleep.

But what does that teach us? It's quite simple: even the resting state itself—that process of recovery after dashing around all day—can only take place *in movement*, even if this is a somewhat different kind of movement than whatever is done while awake.

From the point of view of your motoric ability and connection with your body, this means making your transition into a so-called period of rest a form of *continuous* and so as *unbroken* a movement as possible. You want to sit down? Don't just let yourself drop into a chair or armchair in such a way that your vertebrae shudder. Make every effort to sit down in a *roundabout movement*, thus avoiding any break, which is nothing but an abrupt change of direction.

Moving in this way is not difficult at all and demands no particular extra effort; quite the contrary. Once you have practiced this for a period of time, you will notice that the physical wear and tear and the weariness you otherwise took to be completely normal and acceptable have noticeably diminished. Sitting down is of course just one example. Once you have sat down, it then naturally progresses onwards in terms of *roundabout* movement so that we can now reduce our advice on self-direction to a simple statement: *Always move in an unbroken fashion!*

Will you always succeed? Of course not! You will, though, make the commitment that the real challenge when implementing this as yet unfamiliar way of moving consists less of getting it just right but much more in *correcting yourself* when you deviate away from it. "Failure" therefore is not just pre-programmed—it is even the norm and represents your real adversary. So here comes another maxim: *correct unflinchingly*!

Of course "unflinchingly" in this context means without exception, once again a major demand you can hardly ever meet. That's not absolutely all there is to it, however. Failure and misfiring, making mistakes and defeat in battle can neither be prevented nor removed from existence with a snap of the fingers or through determined practice and the rehearsal of mechanical procedures. Rather it's much more important to go about things correctly (that is, according to your original objective). Distracted again? Taking a break again? Landed too hard on your backside when sitting down? Don't waste time in lingering over a closer examination of these errors or even putting forward any flimsy explanations and excuses for them. Instead: sober correction … and keep going!

The common saying about learning from your mistakes is of course rubbish! What would you want to learn from your mistakes, other than how someone can do something wrong? Clearly you can already do that or you would not have made the mistake in the first place. In American business culture there is an old maxim that says that you can only really measure an entrepreneur's greatness and competence when he or she has gone bankrupt at least three times in their life. For it is not the insolvency and the failure of their business undertakings that are the decisive factor but the fact that he or she stood up again undaunted, did it again, and strove hard to lead the next undertaking to a successful conclusion. In equestrian sports they say that no one can really call themselves real equestrians until they have fallen off their horse at least seven times. You wouldn't wish a neck-breaking fall from some temperamental stallion upon anyone; it is much more a matter of soberly registering the failure, not letting it make any further impression on you, and continuing on the path you have chosen. So: *don't get lost in small battles and don't stop!*

What we're talking about here has nothing to do with doggedness. That's precisely why we always use the word *sober,* here meaning "without showiness" and also excluding making justifications after the event ("that only happened because ..." "if the stirrup hadn't been worn so smooth ..." "I still had the alcohol in my system from the evening before ..." and so on). Registering the failure, the falling short, the mistake itself—yes! Embellishing it further, challenging it, coming up with reasons and excuses—*categorically no!*

Once you have determined that the notion of being able to stand completely motionless in space even for a few minutes is pure self-deception, we can now examine one of the reasons for this: you would immediately tip over were it any other way. And why? Gravity. Precisely, we would always end up being dragged down to the earth's core, and this is only prevented from happening by two factors: the earth's crust, which we aren't able to naturally smash through, and the fact *that we continuously adapt ourselves so that it doesn't happen.* The apparent adjustments we make while standing clearly show this. If we didn't adjust in this way and thus support our centralizing posture, gravity would pull us to the ground.

We are able to support ourselves and we continue to do so for example by leaning on a tabletop, pushing against a doorframe, or sitting on a chair. From gravity's point of view that changes nothing, of course, and so we continually align ourselves against it even when sitting and lying down. The habit is not stupid; it's a basic requirement for life and our survival, something we take no notice of whatsoever and accept as a matter of course, just like breathing.

Clearly, the stillness procedure is not carried out without any resultant wear and tear; the exact opposite is the case. Although we don't register any of it as a rule, this permanent adjustment against gravity is the purest heavy labor. Periods of sleeping and lying down only mitigate it because in doing so we distribute our body weight along the horizontal plane rather than the vertical and may therefore use other parts of the body in the process in contrast to standing, walking, or sitting. Therefore, the recuperative effect of lying and sitting down does not least have something to do with this unloading maneuver. There is still some heavy work that's conducted during this process, and we can see that because these all too drawn out periods of lying prone do wear us down and diminish us so we develop back and sacral pain and even chafe our skin, presenting a serious health hazard especially to bedridden patients.

The "relief" we feel when leaning against static structures like walls, tabletops, chairs, or armchairs is likewise illusory. To achieve it, we must also constantly amend every supposedly comfortable position through minimal or greater movements and through displacement of our body weight. This relief is therefore not genuine, and in order not to break apart under the load, we have to remain in motion all the time. Only through permanent dynamics can we escape the murderous potential for destruction of monolithic stasis.

On top of that, we always fall in the direction we are looking in, to put it simply. Here too is a very subtle and normally completely unconscious adjustment mechanism that can nevertheless be observed clearly when we look more closely. With a more intense gaze, we can also observe this with colleagues and friends, in pedestrian zones and in the subway. In reality, people self-align en masse toward each other, in so far as they are located within a common range of perception, whereas gravity naturally keeps insisting on a centralizing self-alignment. Put briefly, we always plunge toward each other.

Now the ultimate realization of these rushing movements would naturally mean us relentlessly bouncing against each other, ending in collisions. But this usually only happens by accident, as—when the time comes—we always adjust ourselves away from such impact, to avoid collisions. The fact that continual clashes of this kind would neither be especially practical nor socially acceptable needs no further elaboration here.

What's really happening is only apparent as soon as you strive successfully for as autonomous a movement as possible in which you still have to keep dealing with gravity but don't align yourself any more against other people in your immediate surroundings. This is entirely possible; however, it requires you to constantly apply your highest attentiveness to your way of moving. In actuality you only need to withdraw your "falling upon someone else" and shift to your own vertical. There's really no more to say about this technique. Depending on the degree of control, you can then arrive at the most spectacular outcomes. For example, it is an easy thing to take others, who up to this point albeit unconsciously, are steering their way into a collision with you under your physical directive control or even to hurl them through space without any contact. Such things are often addressed by the inner styles of the (mostly Asian) martial arts. And although in this particular field one claim is often no better or worse than another, seeing that people persistently like to draw attention to themselves, generally speaking these effects are well vouched for and thoroughly genuine.

So much for basic physical training! The comments above cover everything you need to know about it at this present moment in time plus some pointers regarding practical implementation. Should you not believe yourself capable of realizing this on your own, you are then of course free to engage with the inner styles of martial arts. You could, for example, visit a suitable martial arts school and take part in regular lessons there. Just make sure also that an *inner* style is really being taught and not an outer one. The outer styles as a rule don't get involved with this form of subtle motor skills and directing of movement.

In this context we recommend from personal experience the Russian *Systema*, which is now being offered in many urban centers. One of the great advantages of Systema lies in its extremely sober pragmatism that renounces all metaphysics and the dubious postulation of any "subtle energies" such as chi, for example. There is nothing secretive about Systema, which was originally developed by Russian special forces. Even the name is simple; it means "system." There are no flowery foundation myths and fables of any greatest of enlightened masters who were once attacked on some lonely mountain trail by a band of brigands who were defeated with bare hands, only then to make the repentant leader into their favorite pupil at a later stage. Systema does not require such a fairy tale. The effects it thus produces are fantastic enough! You can find all sorts of video material on the Internet that you can use to form an excellent initial impression. Then you'll probably want to find out for yourself about the real thing, and that's thoroughly recommended. You will find Systema contact details in the appendix.

Mind: Inquiries to Take You Further

In the mystical as well as esoteric bodies of literature you will always find detailed references about how harmful it would be for someone to limit themselves to their ego, to wait upon it and to want to embody it. The reason? It's really much better to connect with the Godhead, the cosmic principle, or the universal energy flow. Just so there's no misunderstanding, many of these works are well intended and some of them are very much worth reading and useful for your life practice. However, there are also countless writings on this subject, and many unfortunately only sow confusion. The preoccupation with the "I" or ego will often be condemned out of hand as a form of morally objectionable egoism with which Judeo-Christian notions of humility will resonate whether by their own admission or not. The New Testament, with its "Yet not my will but yours be done, Lord," is eagerly cited. Behind it stands a "You are nothing, your God is everything" ideology of submission; often all that affected behavior only flows into priggish miserabilism.

As we are concerned here with neither religion nor morals and ethics, we prefer a somewhat more level-headed consideration of the ego. It is certainly no exaggeration to speak of the "ego project" humanity has been pledged to for quite some time. Even in rather more collectively oriented societies with so-called natural or primitive peoples we can observe the ego and its consequences in action. Although individualism is not so strongly pronounced there as in our culture, phenomena like love, hate, jealousy, envy, greed, and conflict over resources are anything but alien to these people.

So it can be observed that the development of the ego, even under the most diverse social and civilizational frameworks, is more or less subject to the same laws. Certainly hunter-gatherer societies, which also tend to be nomadic, require considerable social cohesion where the individual, with his or her wishes, instincts, and desires that might deviate from the group's, enjoys minimal consideration. But if the collective has to secure its resources using the utmost effort (the hunting and gathering of food is ultimately not a mere pastime, but an extremely strenuous and never-ending enterprise), this will of course apply just as much, if not much more, to the individual member of such a community. Also, the individual will ultimately demand a share of the resources they need for survival. And so personal names and identities now represent separate addressees who now expect their own claims for maintenance to be taken into consideration. The spoils of the hunt must now be divvied up regardless of whether they are in fair proportions. Only when the survival of the individual has been sufficiently guaranteed can the community also rely on his or her active participation.

So why these observations when we no longer live in a hunter-gatherer society? Well, as the current state-of-the-art neurology never tires of stressing, the human brain has not evolved significantly since the dawn of *Homo sapiens*. After all, evolutionary processes take time. Even a few million years form much too short a span to expect fundamental biological changes or even expansions in capacity. In other words, our brain, at least in terms of its basic functioning, is still at the same level of development as our club- and spear-wielding forebears. The fact that today we can tackle highly complex areas of knowledge such as quantum physics, genetics, or probability theory does not change anything either. Across this span of time we have still not shed the costume of our instincts and Stone Age reflexes, and the ego can also be identified as one of these archaic survival strategies.

Whatever might once have been (and still today) used as authority to secure individual access to scarce resources turns out on closer analysis to be purely reactive and insubstantial, nothing more than a mere social survival strategy. This leads us back to mysticism and to the whole body of wisdom teachings and ancient religions. With one voice these all attribute only a minor value to the ego, actually classifying it as a human aberration. Granted, this will often happen on various grounds, including unfortunately the safeguarding of the supremacy of social elites such as monarchs, nobility, priesthood, and so on. The care and consolidation of the ego was of course often entirely incumbent upon the ruling castes, not upon their subjects, and certainly not the serfs or the slaves who for the most part were denied their humanity anyway so they could be treated like objects or things. Incidentally, this outlook has not disappeared entirely from the earth despite the official abolition of slavery in the nineteenth century. It was with good reason that Karl Marx spoke of the reification of human beings.

Yet despite these limitations and relativisms, it can be asserted that the "wise ones" of entire world cultures gave rather poor grades to the Ego Project and advised their followers not to get mixed up in it. The historical Buddha was able to accomplish this the most astutely when he elaborated with great clarity upon the completely illusory character of the ego, making every effort to dissuade his followers from continuing to be taken in by the nonsense of competitiveness, a thing to which the development of the ego is indebted.

It should then be easy, then, to put an end to it all with the admonition: "Release yourself from your ego!" There shouldn't really be any more to say than that … except that it would be just as illusory to believe that this could be ended in any singular moment via some short and assertive act of will. For that reason, I recommended that as part of your basic training, you first of all address the question of what your "I" really is. Where does it come from? What does it look like exactly? What conditions does it need in order to exist? Has it changed in the past ten years? In the past twenty? Is that "I" of your childhood still the same as today's? If so, what do they have in common? Memories, perhaps? If so, what else is there? And if not, how are they both different? Are there areas of overlap? If so, where?

And should you arrive at the conclusion that your childhood "I" doesn't really have much in common with your adult "I" of today, then explore the question of whether it's really sensible (with this going on in the background) to speak of a stable, unchanging, and thus *enduring* "I." Is that "I" an absolutely clear-cut entity? (We can see that the old question, "Who am I?" is anything but a trivial one.) What exactly is gained with an "I?" And what would be lost if you didn't have one (anymore)?

Make a list of your interests. This is meant quite literally and should not be limited to your hobbies and leisure pursuits. An interest in food as it serves your metabolism belongs there just as much as an interest in physical integrity, in secure accommodation, in friendships and intimate relationships, in maintaining life, and more. Take your time with it. You can take more than one day to make your list. The important thing is that the list is as comprehensive as possible when you have finished doing it, even if it turns out to be correspondingly long. But set yourself a time limit anyway, one that you won't overstep. Whether it's three days or two weeks, take as long as you determine in advance and stick to it firmly. Experience has shown that anything else will only lead to distraction and fragmentation.

Now consider this list in every detail and keep asking yourself whether you really need an ego to safeguard your interests and, if the answer is yes, how exactly. Should you come to the conclusion (and we are most definitely *not* telling you here that you have to) that this can all be realized without the postulate of an ego, we recommend then that in the future you concern yourself only with the safeguarding of your interests without getting lost in long-winded self-definitions and ego-articulations. Look upon this as a leisurely process of self-detachment at the end of which your ego/I retreats into the background and eventually disappears completely from the screen surface.

Should you come to the conclusion that the ego is still indispensable for your survival at least for the time being, figure out for yourself what it looks like in detail and whether it might be possible to reduce the ego-share of your conscious life bit by bit, naturally without damaging your quality of life at all in the process.

In fact, the ego represents a strategy for becoming depressed, and it only generates an increase in control or power on a superficial level. This at least is what the great wisdom teachings of the East and West also are trying to tell us. You do not have to accept this notion uncritically and without questioning, but you should nevertheless give it a critical appreciation.

Soul: Uncomplicated Effectiveness
Sigil Magic
We have already brought out a detailed introduction to the whole subject of sigil magic elsewhere (*High Magic*, see Sources). For our purposes, here is a shortened account, trimmed down to the essentials.

With regard to sigil magic as developed by Austin Osman Spare, it's principally an issue of circumventing the psychological censor so that tasks or "commands" can be implanted in the unconscious which it can then execute and realize without our active and conscious assistance. This is carried out using the following four steps:

1. Written formulation of a statement of will (the "magical task")

2. Conversion of the letters in the statement of will into an abstract glyph (the actual "sigil")

3. Charge/activation of the sigil

4. Forgetting the sigil (better still: forgetting the entire operation)

According to Freudian teachings that influenced Spare, the intra-psychic censor only allows a very limited amount of direct communication between consciousness/the ego and the subconscious, hence the need for concealment by "transcoding" information into an individual and abstract artwork—the sigil. For this reason the uploading or activation of the sigil is carried out via a light trance, weakening the resistance of the censor. Through the final targeted forgetting of the sigil (or if possible, the entire operation), the censor is in turn prevented from bringing in any possible resistance to the process originating from the superego and any corresponding blocks to it moving into manifestation.

Technically, it could be described as an act of deliberate psychological repression and a precise reversal of what Sigmund Freud wanted to bring into the open with his psychoanalysis. To Freud it was a matter of dragging the repressed contents of the psyche (e.g., early childhood traumas) into consciousness and thus dissolving them. In this way, neuroses and neurotic-compulsive behaviors can be repaired within the framework of psychoanalytical therapy.

The setup with Spare is exactly the other way round. By means of the controlled repression of one's own avowed aims, the subconscious mind can thus be obliged to orient itself upon them and realize these very aims. Used correctly, sigils become an integral component of your organism that for its part works with all the power and energy of its cells to ensure that they are converted to the desired outcomes. According to Spare's conception, "sigils will flesh" by bringing about the outward manifestation of what you desire. To make this happen with the help of sigil magic, you only need a sheet of paper and a pencil. And afterwards not only can you simply forget what happened, you are *even supposed to!* On the path of conventional magic, it really doesn't get any less complicated than this.

The advantage of this approach lies more than anything in the fact that it is on the one hand highly efficient and on the other requires minimum effort. To do it, you need no extensive magical accessories and not even any practical experience in the ways of magic. There are also no statements of belief expected of you, concerning perhaps the existence of deities and spiritual beings or even the theoretical possibility of magical outcomes. You can also understand the whole process in a straightforward way as a psychological operation and keep the term "magic" out of it completely, if that's what you'd prefer. All this does not detract from the effectiveness of sigil magic.

Now let's look at the practical approach using a concrete example. To do this, you should first determine your aim and formulate a corresponding statement of will. This should be as clear and one-pointed as possible. Avoid ambiguous and vague formulations as well as overly specific ones. Aims/statements of will such as "I want everything always to go well in my life" or "I want to win exactly $27,054.37 in the lottery on September 18" as a rule remain unsuccessful. The subconscious can't and won't work toward what it cannot understand. For the best formulation, there are unfortunately no tailor-made rules and templates; you must rely mainly on your intuition.

When you formulate "I want to become rich," this can mean a lottery win or the death of your favorite aunt and inheriting her cottage ... or that you become "rich in experience" as well, perhaps by falling for a con artist who fobs you off with "dead cert" options on the Afghan railway system that ultimately turn out to be toxic assets. And anyway, the desired effect might show up only thirty years later, if ever, making it too vague or ambiguous.

The demand for one-pointedness is easier to fulfill, as it only means that the statement of will should be directed upon one goal and not formulated in too general a manner.

When sigil magic is frequently deployed, it's recommended to have the statement of will always prefaced by the same formulaic opening phrase, for example "I wish that…" or "This is my will, that…" In this way you condition the unconscious with the formula to become active automatically as soon as a new sigil is delivered.

Avoid formulating your statements of will in the following ways:

1. Negative formulations. Namely, these will for the most part be ignored by the unconscious and thus transformed into the opposite. "I don't want to get ill" will quickly become a fatal "I want to get ill." Formulate as positively as possible: "I want to stay well."

2. Abstractions, foreign words, and overcomplicated formulations, unless these have already passed over into your flesh and blood (here meant quite literally) through your job or otherwise well-established pursuit. The unconscious mind of the average person cannot get very far with "diphenylacetone" or "epistemology"

whereas the unconscious of a chemist or a philosophy student is more likely to. Nevertheless, to be on the safe side you should always give preference to a clear and simple formulation.

3. Aims beyond the personal that unequivocally over-step their own effect horizon. Sigil magic is indeed much more effective than people often believe, but there is no way that it's all-powerful, just as your unconscious isn't either. To want to deliver sigils for "world peace," "ending climate change," or "eradicating international terrorism" is an utter overestimation of one's abilities and therefore doomed to failure. You are better off saving yourself the frustration.

The question of whether a statement of will is actually viable or not can only itself be clarified unambiguously and with absolute certainty by the operation's success. In case of doubt, you should then rely above all on your intuition.

Creating the Sigil

This is the simplest and least complicated aspect of sigil magic. Let's take as an example a concern from everyday work: "Next week I want to be praised by my boss." (The time specification facilitates the later evaluation of its success.)

Firstly, the statement of will is written on a piece of paper in capital letters:

NEXT WEEK I WANT TO BE PRAISED BY MY BOSS

Where appropriate, write numbers as words. Don't use punctuation marks like commas, periods, exclamation marks, etc.

Now every letter that appears more than once is crossed out from its second appearance onwards, so that each appears only once:

NEXT WEEK I ~~WANT TO~~ BE ~~PRAISED~~ ~~BY~~ MY ~~BOSS~~

So these are left:

N, E, X, T, W, K, I, A, O, B, P, R, S, D, Y, M

We will now make a sigil out of this collection of letters (see Figure 1).

ICHMLNAESTOVMFGBRD

Figure 1: The first version of the sigil

Here we have simply lined the letters up in a row in a graphic form. A sigil really should not be too complicated so that it doesn't overwhelm the unconscious. On the other hand, it mustn't be too simple either, because this hinders the requisite forgetting once the operation has been carried out. A simple square or circle would simply be too hard to forget. In addition, all the letters used should on closer inspection be recognizable in the sigil, at least hypothetically. In the process of simplification of the sigil, it should also be made somewhat abstract. For example, this could look like Figure 2.

Figure 2: The simplified, abstracted sigil

As you will see without difficulty, we have taken a bit away from the basic sigil but have also added some material. All the same, we can still continue to trace in it the complete letters from our list above, even if it is a little tricky. One traced line, that is, can also include several letters at the same time and is also valid when the letter is upside down. For example, the curve can work both as an O and a C. The letters W, K, N, A, E, and so on can also be picked out once again without much difficulty in the finished sigil.

You can now embellish the sigil a little to lend it a "more magical" appearance, as is illustrated in Figure 3.

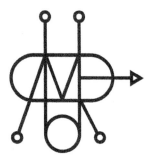

Figure 3: The finished, embellished sigil

The circle and triangle of the embellishment have no meaning of their own; they merely serve in making the finished sigil look like a re-created medieval sigil form, purely a matter of taste. When creating sigils, you don't need any artistic talent. In fact, sigils can prove to be even more effective when they look somewhat wooden or primitive as explained earlier, that the unconscious associates a roughly hewn appearance with base instincts and energies. With time you will probably develop your own distinctive sigil style, but of course every individual sigil should exhibit its own individual imprint so it cannot be mistaken for others.

The finished product is a glyph that has no discernable meaning. Even the crossing out of the redundant letters is a part of the already mentioned coding of the statement of will. The graphic transposition carries this process on in a creative manner. As the magical statement of the will's coding is smuggled undetected past the psychic censor, it consequently does not trigger the locking and blocking mechanisms, allowing the unconscious to go about its work unhindered.

Now you know everything about the technique of sigil manufacture to be able to make successful use of it.

Charging the Sigil

The charging of the finished sigil takes place *spasmodically*, that is, convulsively and jerkily. It is connected to an exertion of energy but permits the required energy to rise up in a variety of ways. Austin Osman Spare recommended what he termed the *death posture* for charging the sigil, but he barely elaborated upon this. Nowadays, most practitioners are in agreement that the aim of the death posture should be to establish as much of an emptying of one's thoughts as possible, even as far as doing so completely. If you can achieve that, the sigil can be loaded unhindered into the unconscious.

The charging process in sigil magic can be compared to a computer program uploaded or fed ("booted up") into the memory of the computer. In other words, the sigil is uploaded *into* the unconscious. We can also just as easily speak of sigil "activation."

In principle, it's of no consequence whatever form of the death posture you choose for activating a sigil. The important thing is that you embark on an adequate emptying of your thoughts. The term "death posture" is in fact based upon the image of the "dying" of thoughts, the temporary extinguishing of consciousness. On that same basis the orgasm is referred to as the "little death." This "death" of mental activity, also known as trance, is accompanied by a transitory dissolution of the ego consciousness, which indeed primarily feeds upon mental activity.

Thought Emptying

Imagine the emptying of your thoughts as being like that condition you are familiar with in moments of extreme anger or joy: a brief state of mind in which the whole of the outside world either concentrates itself into one single point or disappears completely, in either of which at least no reflection upon your own identity continues to take place. This state can be reached particularly quickly via physical stress, a fact demonstrated by the first of the two following techniques for sigil activation.

The Death Posture (I)

Do this while standing or sitting. The sigil is prominently displayed on the wall in front of you or lying on a table. Breathe in deeply and close your mouth, eyes, ears, and nostrils with the fingers of both hands. Now hold your breath until it becomes almost unbearable. But don't relax—instead try to go one step further. While doing so, don't think about the sigil or about your aim. Finally, just before you faint, open your eyes as wide as they will go and while you exhale and fill your lungs with fresh air, stare at the sigil. Then abruptly shut your eyes again and banish the sigil (see the following section, "Banishing the Sigil").

Warning: Don't under any circumstances attempt this technique if you suffer from cardiac arrhythmia, risk of heart attack, damage from lung infection, high blood pressure, or constricted blood vessels. If any of the above applies, please work exclusively with the second technique, as described in the next section, "The Death Posture (II)."

If you want, you can stare at the sigil while you are standing. In doing so, fold and twist your arms in as unnatural a position as possible behind your back, stand on tiptoes and bend backwards, so you can just barely maintain your balance. If you moderate this technique using a somewhat gentler approach to holding your breath, then it is also suitable to a limited extent for people who have the physical complaints described in the warning above.

The Death Posture (II)

This variation upon the death posture is much milder than the first but it works just as well, as long as it's carried out as intensively as it needs to be. It does call for a little more practice, however. It's conducted while seated and is suitable for people with problems with the heart or respiratory system.

The sigil is placed in front of you on the table while you are seated straight-backed and upright, the palms of your hands placed on the table's surface. Your thumbs are splayed out at right angles, your hands are lying flat so that the thumb-tips are touching and the sigil is placed in the open square formed by the space between your hands (see Figure 4 on next page). Stare at the sigil with your eyes wide open and do not close them, even when they start to water a bit.

Now very briefly spasm the muscles of your under thigh, first in one leg and then the other, and then in both at the same time. The spasming should be firm and easy; it is enough for it to last only a split second, but that it should be as intense as possible (so it doesn't bring on a long-term cramp!). Now make sure that the muscle tightening continues in the upper thigh, then through your torso, hands, and arms, and ultimately right up to your scalp. After some practice a "tightening through process" across the whole body will not take more than half a second to implement.

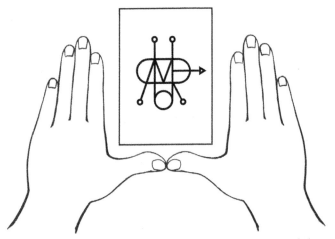

Figure 4: The position of the sigil in the death posture (II)

At the climax of the tightening, open your eyelids even wider, while you are still staring at the sigil, then shut them again abruptly and banish the sigil (see "Banishing the Sigil").

Banishing the Sigil

After activation, the sigil must be banished. This is the first step in forgetting the whole operation. The simplest banishment consists of a large and hearty laugh. It will probably come across as a little bit contrived at first as we are not accustomed in general to laughing out loud on command, but that doesn't matter. Actually, laughter is one of the least complicated approaches to the process of emptying of the thoughts I explained above. (Just try to solve a complicated arithmetical problem while heartily laughing. It's well nigh impossible!)

Ultimately, you can distract yourself after the magical sigil operation by concentrating on something as profane as possible. The less you are dealing with magical concerns or with anything that is even remotely to do with the operation, the better. Therefore, activities like watching television, playing sports, or sitting down with video games are especially good for subsequent distraction. The "channel," leading into the unconscious through trance should be shut down as completely as possible after the uploading process.

The sigil must now be forgotten as soon as possible because otherwise the rational mind—and with it, the psychic censor—can intervene in the process and endanger its execution through doubt, inquisitiveness, or impatience. Ideally, you will forget not only the external form of the sigil and its operation but also its very goal. In practice, unfortunately, this is only rarely achieved without great effort, because in most cases magical operations are preoccupied with concerns, which are quite important to you. It is therefore recommended that in the case of long-term goals you create a number of sigils at the same time and store them together in reserve until you no longer know the purpose for which each respective sigil was intended. Only then do you activate the sigils one after the other.

Should an unwanted sigil re-emerge suddenly from the unconscious, it is activated once again and then banished. However, it often suffices to divert one's attention from the sigil, ideally through laughter, until it has disappeared again.

THE SIGIL FOR SELF-PROTECTION

Once you have amassed a bit of experience with sigil magic, as described above (three or four operations should suffice even for the absolute beginner), you should then customize a sigil for magical self-protection and activate this correctly, of course.

As the sigil itself is also the statement of will made just by you personally so you should formulate it quite individually. For example, it could say: "This is my will, that I am protected from magical attacks" or: "I want my magical protection to be impregnable." If you would like something more drastic but still couched in purely defensive terms, you could also formulate for example: "May whoever attacks me magically be cursed" or similar.

As I have said, these examples should only serve as suggestions. So don't adopt these formulations unaltered, but shape them for yourself in exactly the way you want. Then proceed as described above.

When it comes to a "general sigil" of this importance, it can be useful to wear it on your body in physical form as a talisman (not visibly though; it must still remain forgotten). So you might roll the paper up tightly after the sigil has been charged and dip it in beeswax, so that you could keep it safe in a hollow locket or pendant and then attach that to a necklace. You could also sew the wax-coated rolled-up paper into a piece of black silk and make a pendant out of that.

This, however, is not absolutely necessary and is also not always something to be recommended, in case your new necklace provokes unwanted and intrusive questions from friends, partners, or family members. I just wanted to mention the possibility, because it can be a thoroughly sensible and effective option, depending upon your personal temperament.

Protocols
PROTOCOL CHAPTER 3–1
00.00–01.20 (80') *Phase 1*: Lying down
01.20–01.52 (32') *Phase 2*: Shallow breathing
01.52–02.27 (35') *Phase 3*: Lying down
02.27–03.00 (33') *Phase 4*: Shallow breathing
03.00–04.30 (90') *Phase 5*: Lying down
04.30–05.00 (30') *Phase 6*: Shallow breathing
05.00–06.00 (60') *Phase 7*: Report

Explanations
Lying down. On your back (if necessary slightly skewed to the right), outwardly motionless, alert.

Shallow breathing. Make your breathing as shallow as possible in this lying down position, without becoming tense.

Protocol Chapter 3–2

00.00–01.10 (70') *Phase 1:* Lying down
01.10–01.42 (32') *Phase 2:* Impulse circulation
01.42–02.17 (35') *Phase 3:* Lying down
02.17–03.17 (60') *Phase 4:* Report

Explanations

Lying down. On your back (if necessary slightly skewed to the right), outwardly motionless, alert.

Impulse circulation. Standing up *without any outward body movement* with an immediate return to a lying down position before any bodily reaction occurs.

Protocol Chapter 3–3

00.00–01.00 (60') *Phase 1:* Lying down
01.00–01.06 (6') *Phase 2:* Stand—Applying pressure 100%
01.06–01.12 (6') *Phase 3:* Stand—Applying pressure 50%
01.12–01.18 (6') *Phase 4:* Stand—Applying pressure 33%
01.18–02.08 (50') *Phase 5:* Lying down
02.08–02.14 (6') *Phase 6:* Stand—Applying pressure 25%
02.14–02.26 (12') *Phase 7:* Shallow breathing
02.26–03.26 (60') *Phase 8:* Report

Explanations

Lying down. On your back (if necessary slightly skewed to the right), outwardly motionless, alert.

1. *Applying pressure 100 percent.* In an upright position, legs shoulder width apart, clasping an object in both hands and holding it clear in front of your body without being supported by anything. This is first of all carried out with normal pressure to maintain a (subjective) reference value of 100 percent expenditure of pressure.

2. *Applying pressure 50 percent.* Just like point one, but with half the amount of pressure expenditure (50 percent) in relation to the previously established reference value.

3. *Applying pressure 33 percent.* Just like point one, but with one-third the amount of pressure expenditure (33 percent) in relation to the previously established reference value.

4. *Applying pressure 25 percent.* Just like point one, but with one quarter the amount of pressure expenditure (25 percent) in relation to the previously established reference value.

It is recommended that you should use as the object perhaps an unbreakable plastic bottle filled with fresh water, which has been tightly closed beforehand. This will help in the event of letting the object slip and will avoid broken shards and resultant injuries as well as other damage.

It will turn out that over time the bottle will threaten to slip out of your hands. In fact, the use of a "deep grip" (that is, by using an ever stronger pressure) will also not permanently stop this process. ("In the depths, the grip gets lost.") For that reason, it's a matter of abandoning pressure exertion if possible when you are holding on and, instead, of developing an alternative form of grip.

Tip: Do your best to work with gravity, rather than against it.

Shallow breathing. Make your breathing as shallow as possible in this lying down position, without becoming tense.

PROTOCOL CHAPTER 3–4
00.00–00.25 (25') *Phase 1:* Lying down
00.25–00.35 (10') *Phase 2:* Shallow breathing
00.35–01.35 (60') *Phase 3:* Lying down
01.35–02.15 (40') *Phase 4:* Impulse circulation
02.15–03.45 (90') *Phase 5:* Lying down
03.45–03.50 (05') Phase 6: Standing—
  Applying pressure 100%
03.50–04.00 (10') Phase 7: Standing—
  Applying pressure 25%
04.00–04.22 (22') *Phase 8:* Lying down
04.22–04.55 (33') *Phase 9:* Shallow breathing
04.55–05.10 (15') *Phase 10:* Lying down
05.10–05.25 (15') *Phase 11:* Impulse circulation
05.25–05.35 (10') *Phase 12:* Lying down

05.35–06.10 (35') *Phase 13:* Marking your boundaries L

06.10–06.45 (35') *Phase 14:* Note taking while walking around

06.45–07.35 (50') *Phase 15:* Lying down

07.35–08.35 (60') *Phase 16:* Report

Explanations

Lying down. On your back (if necessary slightly skewed to the right), outwardly motionless, alert.

Shallow breathing. Make your breathing as shallow as possible in this lying down position, without becoming tense.

Impulse circulation. Standing up *without any outward body movement* with an immediate return to a lying down position before any bodily reaction occurs.

1. *Applying pressure 100 percent.* In an upright position, legs a shoulder width apart, clasping an object in both hands and holding it clear in front of your body, without being supported by anything. This is first of all carried out with normal pressure, to maintain a (subjective) reference value of 100 percent expenditure of pressure.

2. *Applying pressure 25 percent.* Just like point one, but with one quarter the amount of pressure expenditure (25 percent) in relation to the previously established reference value.

It is recommended that you should use as the object perhaps an unbreakable plastic bottle filled with fresh water, which has been tightly closed beforehand. This will help in the event of letting the object slip and will avoid broken shards and resultant injuries as well as other damage.

It will turn out that over time the bottle will threaten to slip out of your hands. In fact, the use of a "deep grip" (that is, by using an ever stronger pressure) will also not permanently stop this process. ("In the depths, the grip gets lost.") For that reason, it's a matter of abandoning pressure exertion if possible when you are holding on and instead of developing an alternative form of grip.

Tip: Do your best to work with gravity, rather than against it.

Marking your boundaries L. A precise assessment takes place in the lying down position, of where the "alien" and "home" begin and continue on. While doing it, you begin at first with the body. The relevant areas are then also extended, as the case may be. In the note taking and reporting phases, the results are then documented in a schematic and graphic sketch.

Note taking while walking around. For this protocol, you abandon your original position and work while standing or walking. You can walk up and down the room or visit the toilet, etc. This helps with the production of additional self-alignment possibilities once you have returned to your lying down position.

In addition to that, you can use the time to make written notes, draw sketches, etc., which you can draw upon for hints at the end of the overall summing up in your reporting session.

4

SELF-PROTECTION BEGINS WITH YOURSELF

Recognizing and Ending Self-Destructive Habits

Body: Recognizing Body Routines and Ending Them

The brain creates routines to conserve effort and energy in which it establishes patterns where perception is not helpful and self-reflexive, memorized answers are offered up in the face of new and emerging issues without careful *a priori* analysis. The body has similar set routines it falls into, usually without our conscious intervention. Think of the digestion and excretion cycles we are subject to or our sleep patterns, as well as the manner in which we adjust our gait or pick up and move objects.

A routine is primarily a good thing in as much as it reduces all kinds of expenditure, including the amount of required energy. Expenditure is always a good deal greater with tasks that aren't routine, mental or physical. But here we find the drawback: routines (physical and mental) do not get updated and adapted to specific situations. For example, if someone has to navigate their way carefully through their neighborhood with a broken leg after a ski accident, they will have developed a walking routine in the process, even if it's just temporary, but it'll be no longer necessary once the cast has been removed. Nevertheless it can often take a long time before it is replaced again by the earlier "normal" way of getting around. When it comes to long-term routines often ingrained over years and decades, any change demands a high cost. So what might once have seemed right and fitting in the past, like holding your tongue when an authority figure imparted some of their knowledge to you or going easy on the leg affected by a stubborn knee injury, might often prove counterproductive or even harmful under other altered circumstances.

What bodily routines can you identify yourself? How do you place your feet on the ground while you are walking? Do you roll over the balls of your feet or do you drag the soles along the surface of the ground like a flatiron? Which leg do you put more weight on? Which arm? Do you suffer from any kind of poor posture you might fix by aligning your shoulders and spine differently? When sitting down, do you let yourself fall down into furniture so that it creaks? (Have you already forgotten the relevant advice in chapter 2 perhaps?) If so: what would it be like if you tried a softer and gentler way of landing that involved less impact, if only for a few weeks? While walking, do you let your arms swing like pendulous weights? Have you ever tried to move through a space with your upper body as upright as possible and as still as you can and without swinging your arms *and* without getting cramped in the process but with as comfortable a demeanor as possible ... even a "cozy" one?

How do you pick things up, whether they are heavy or light? Do you lift them up with a jerk, putting great pressure on your sacral region and spine? Have you ever tried to sort yourself out while under pressure to do something like pick up a beer barrel, a heavy suitcase, or some fully laden shopping bags? How do you set the table? Do you put the dishes and cutlery down at their place on the table with a firm pressure, maybe with an expenditure of energy which could be reduced comfortably, meaning with the same outcome but without any collision reverberation? Have you ever tried to perform every movement that you are aware of with significantly less effort, including extra attempt at a smooth seamlessness?

Our aims are not just about putting an end to every physical routine; some of them should still be very useful and meaningful for you. However, they all need to be put to the test on a regular basis, because that's the only way you can ensure that you optimize your self-alignment and reduce avoidable wear and tear as much as you can. Thus you increase not only your physical resilience but also contribute toward the strengthening of your personal integrity in all fields.

Without any doubt, facial expressions can be classified with other physical habits and routines that barely see reflection. And like your bodily posture, facial expressions are in no way simply passive and inferior expressions of feelings. In fact, they have much more of an effect on the positive determination of one's emotional condition or frame of mind. The fact that psychology finally discovered this toward the end of the last century and proved it experimentally has obstructed that knowledge of this has had an impression upon theatrical performance, rhetoric, and ritual and cult worship for centuries.

Your smile might be the expression of your good mood. Conversely, you can also thoroughly banish a bad mood by assuming a smile, even if at first it feels somewhat contrived. Are you feeling miserable? Don't feel too great? Are you angry or irritable? If so, put on a smile and try and keep it going. By doing this, you might not be able to alleviate a heavy feeling of depression, but you can thoroughly attenuate and even completely dissolve the occasional dip in mood, bouts of melancholy, and self-destructive negativity.

Does that sort of fake smiling rub you the wrong way? Internal objections may arise, such as "What's the point of all that play-acting?" "That's just dishonest/artificial/insincere!" "I won't distort myself," "I would come across as foolish." If so let it be, but you should be quite aware that it is clearly more important to you to indulge your current mood and your routine ways of expressing yourself, rendering you at their mercy and dependent upon them than to take over the decision-making responsibility yourself for how you are feeling. As any experienced actor can tell you, a focused exercising of influence over your facial expressions and physical posture can have an unmistakable effect on your feelings and your mood. Even your thought processes—which in reality are definitely not "independent" from your bodily self-orientation—will be greatly influenced in the process.

In addition, your own capability for facial movement and expression works like a kind of antenna that allows you to pick up and affect the mood of another. You can prove that quickly for yourself by observing what is going on inside you when you describe to someone a problem you just had to deal with. How do you react if this person assumes a bored expression, avoids your gaze, or stares transfixed at something else? What if the person returns your gaze, signals interest by widening their eyes, reflects back to you through the mouth and lips feelings such as despondency, dismay, joy, or serenity depending on what you have just been talking about? In fact, when we are having conversations we are incessantly busy (even if almost always on an unconscious level) inwardly scanning the facial expressions, gestures, and overall demeanor of our interlocutors to see how they react to us, how they stand in relation to us, and whether we should trust them, rely on them, or if we would be better off distancing ourselves from them. Communication is a complete package by no means restricted to the spoken word. The term "body language" would seem to serve as proof.

In your conversations with others, it will be of great advantage to pay attention to every relevant facial expression and physical orientation (which by the way will mean that people will be much more open with you). Should you want to ward off both direct and hidden attacks or better still, not even allow them to surface in the first place, you should definitely strive to maintain the fullest possible control over your facial expressions, gestures, and posture. You won't need to take acting lessons, even though they might be thoroughly useful. For our purposes, it really will be enough to act out certain moods from time to time in front of the mirror and to try playing them accompanied by various expressions. We certainly all did it as children, but unfortunately with advancing age it became embarrassing to us or adults simply drove it out of us. Today, though, you can go ahead and do it without any witnesses— you won't have to look foolish in front of anyone!

What kinds of smiles do you have in your repertoire? Which one has an exaggerated effect, and which is too weak or too subtle? Which is your most heartfelt smile? How do you produce a mocking one? An amused smirk? A self-satisfied grin? How do you look at something to signal genuine interest? How do you convey the fact that you are bored? Pay attention to your eyes. Which is a direct look and which an indirect? When you ask a question, do you raise your eyebrows? If so, how high exactly? How do you convey consternation? Terror? Empathic concern? Confidence? Pensiveness? Can you create a look of avarice with your face?

Jealousy? Bewilderment? Farsightedness? Superiority? Inferiority? Anxiety? Sorrow?

There are countless forms of expression, signals, and messages we convey just by using our facial expressions that are usually completely automatic and unconscious. Our aim here is not controlling every bit of self-expression down to the smallest detail and producing them to order. We are not robots, and even a professional actor does not play a role all the time. But by extending your grip on these means of expression in social settings, you'll be able to assume significantly more influence over both your own state of mind as well as over that of your interlocutor without having to take lessons in rhetoric, training in reasoning, and behavioral coaching either.

When you have worked your way through a complete palette of forms of expression as sketched briefly above (which by the way costs no time at all and can also be a lot of fun to do) you can try rapidly changing from one facial expression to the next to make the whole process even more dynamic. Naturally, pairs of opposites are good options: joy/anger, cheerfulness/displeasure, delight/horror, interest/boredom, and so on.

The last element we must address is the expressions' accompanying bodily postures. You can try various poses: stiff standing to attention, slumped with head hanging, pushing your chin out, raised shoulders, dropped shoulders, chest pushed out, calm looseness, being ready to pounce, rigid immobility, and so on.

Now follows the synchronization of facial expression and bodily posture: (simulated) laughter, (simulated) crying; an attitude of flight, an attitude of attack; aggression and peacefulness; sympathy and apathy. Expression itself occurs as facial expression or physical movement, but neither in isolation. It's more often the case that both are usually coordinated with each other. Of course we don't have just one single correct version because everyone has their own style. The states of mind being represented are themselves defined with differing levels of intensity and can interpret many nuances. See to it that you handle the synchronization in a natural way and perhaps effect corrections and modifications where necessary to produce the desired expression in a more targeted fashion.

As a parallel, you can likewise observe other people and discover how they express their emotions. Of course you shouldn't stare at people in an intimidating manner as if they are fascinating laboratory animals—you definitely won't end up making any friends that way. A short and attentive glance will usually suffice to give you enough information about what's going on with the other person and how that person has facially and physically brought it about. It might be that here and there you can learn something new. Perhaps whatever you learn will enable you to start using the self-expression techniques yourself. Perhaps your observations might also show you several more off-putting examples that you would prefer not to use yourself.

Once you feel reasonably secure in this area, you can have a go at experimenting with others, for example, by performing contradictory outward movements, just so you can observe their reactions. So if you signal some sort of joy through your bodily posture, but then suffering through your facial expression, this can then—provided it's been carried out smartly and convincingly—sometimes trigger odd reactions in others. We don't want to anticipate anything here or awake any expectations with a list of possible effects, as these could possibly just mislead you. Because with this form of trying to influence others or, perhaps even more important, of defense against their respective attempts to influence you, it always unfolds in a very individual way. For that reason you can't put forward any rigid rules or laws about it. All the same, you shouldn't try out these experiments on people who are closest to you and to whom you are personally very important. Because then you could easily trigger an indeterminate unease, which they often won't be able to place properly, and thus ultimately forfeit their trust and destroy relationships without meaning to.

Mind: Why (According to Einstein) an Atom Is Easier to Crack Than a Prejudice— and How You Can Overcome This Mechanism

Every form of self-protection begins with your self. Before you can effectively resist the challenges and dangers coming in from outside, you have to put your own house in order, as they say. In military strategy as well as in the realm of interpersonal relationships, it's very often the case that it's not the enemy's attacks and superior strength that tip the balance in a conflict, but much more one's own weaknesses and short-comings that only require deft exploitation by the opposing party in order to force a defeat. For example, that person who happens to be naïve, uninformed, and in an unworldly way tied up in a clique of amoral cynics shouldn't be surprised when they re-emerge wounded from this situation. Not infrequently people talk utterly recklessly only because they pay no attention to their surroundings, the nature and mechanics of which they don't adequately appraise. They might project their own values unquestioningly upon others and thus hand themselves over to the knife, as it were. Whoever passes the time in a milieu full of tough guys who prefer to communicate with their fists instead of engaging in rational discussion and tries to assert himself or herself with the inadequate resources offered by rhetoric will under certain circumstances be better taught by getting a swift black eye.

As any defense lawyer will tell you, the sheer fear of uniformed state power can often make a significant difference to the statements dragged out of the accused during a police interview or in the course of an early morning police raid on their house that they bitterly regret later on in court.

Ignorance, lack of interest in world developments and social mechanics, self-infatuation and blindness to the concerns and interests of others—none of these are things we mean to appraise here morally but from a technical point of view they are merely self-defeating weaknesses and short-comings that could in most cases be deactivated without any great effort. The only precondition for this is an ability for sober self-criticism coupled with the resolve to undertake everything necessary to rectify one's own weaknesses and shortcomings or—where this perhaps cannot be achieved—to align one's own behavior accordingly. This is by no means impossible and can even be accomplished with very little effort. So there is no rational reason not to do so.

It is often the case of course that people generally don't perceive their own weaknesses as such, treating them instead like the most normal things in the world. With a little effort, even that can be thoroughly put right via rational and unbiased contemplation. Not infrequently, however, you will have to take into consideration the opinions of family and close friends, perhaps even of experienced professional consultants. Certainly, even your best friend will always only see you through their own glasses; your closest girlfriend might misjudge many aspects of you and completely grab the wrong end of the stick. All of it can be put to the test, however. In this case it is not a question of subjecting yourself uncritically to others' judgment but to develop and sharpen your own critical faculties.

Among the greatest dangers are self-destructive habits and especially the ones you don't recognize or whose significance remains hidden from you for ages until it is too late. A not inconsiderable part of contemporary journalism and politics is focused on extending supposedly well-intentioned advice to people whether they want it or (usually) not. And where necessary you'll also be patronized by laws, rules, and regulations "for your own benefit." The current industry of doling out advice is actually anything but new; it's just that the priesthood and the ruling classes previously carried out such activities. In reality it is always the best option to be a sovereign human being or to develop into one—a person who will never be omniscient and certainly not omnipotent, but who is always capable at least of containing and safeguarding his or her own borders before they break out of them in due course. Another aspect of this is that when necessary, you should take the help of others in consideration. In this respect the goal is to become as self-sufficient as possible and not hand over the direction of your own life to others.

What "bad" habits do you have? Why do you classify them as bad in the first place? Which are your "good" habits? Why do you consider them good? Do the people around you see things exactly the same way? If your answer is yes, are you really absolutely sure of that? Have you ever asked them? And if they don't see things that way, what criticisms do they mount against them? And just between us, in what ways might they even be right? Once you have finally recognized bad habits and have also for the sake of clarity put them down in writing, ask yourself what you can do about them. (You can and should of course destroy these records later on so they don't fall into the wrong hands.) Does it seem hopeless to you in some cases? Perhaps it's because you failed at it so often already in the past. Consider what exactly you've done about it and what you might have tried up to this point. How would it be with a completely new approach that might up to now have been utterly unfamiliar to you? Are there other people who have had to struggle with the same problem? Could you perhaps learn something from them, even if it's only how someone really shouldn't do it? Or might they be able to help you with it in an immediate and direct way?

Have you ever given good advice to others that you yourself might have been better off following but you never did so? How will you come to terms with your weaknesses in the future? Will you accept them with a shrug of the shoulders? Or are you ready to take them on with persistent patience instead of always expecting to be able to deal with them overnight using a quick-fix approach?

By the way, hanging out with the wrong sort of people can also be counted as one of your detrimental and self-destructive habits. Do you have "friends" who only ever exploit you but are never there for you even if you need help from them? What use are they to you? Consider people who only criticize you (even if they may often happen to be right) and never build you up, only sometimes giving you a few grudging words of encouragement—will you actually continue to tolerate them in your life? What about that leech of a colleague who although he constantly flatters you and praises you to the skies, immediately draws in his praise anxiously and stabs you in the back just when it starts to look like you have fallen out of favor with the boss?

Of course you can't choose your workplace colleagues. What you can do is treat them in a thoroughly friendly manner and keep them at a certain distance and refuse them an unwanted and opportunistic solidarity. Out of the goodness of your heart, will you still water the plants of your dear neighbor while she is on holiday, even though there is proof that she constantly talks about you behind your back? Break free from this connection! Don't end things with disputes unless you want to set in motion even more protracted and annoying conflicts. Respectful aloofness and the maintenance of several plausible excuses are usually enough to rid yourself effectively of the human parasites in your life without smashing too much crockery or burning any bridges.

Please note that we are talking here about *your own* conduct, not of an intention to change others or show them a different way. It's not even true that one can simply talk about everything with everyone. Many people are not amenable to such conversations, and it would only be a bad and self-destructive habit on your part, to always let yourself be misled by this delusion of looking to have a "reasonable" conversation, when on the opposing side only lack of interest, lethargy, misunderstanding, or even hostile malice prevail.

At this point I should mention that what's written above is about very careful and mild reflection in addition to behavior. Certainly there are other ways as well. Many magical and spiritual schools advise a pupil to shed every (yes, *absolutely every single*) habit without replacing them with new ones. An extreme example: the *Aghori babas*, the *Kaula* tantrics, and the Sadhus of India lead lives not only of extreme asceticism but also do things that go way beyond situations that would send shivers up the spines of normal people. These adepts prefer to spend their time near the cremation grounds, only live off what people donate to them, consume waste including feces and flesh from rotting corpses, often eat their food only out of human skulls, sometimes copulate on human carcasses and do pretty much everything that has brought the so-called left-hand path of tantra into disrepute in India far more than in the West. Mad? Asocial? Psychotic and perverse? Not at all! Because their guiding spiritual principle tells them: Everything is divine, everything is equally good, squeamishness is only an expression of human ignorance. You can find among them illiterate peasants; former university professors, doctors, and scholars of the highest level of learning; members of the middle class merchant castes; people both young and old. Above all, one thing is common to all of them: they want nothing to do with religious dogma, social conventions, and their own comfortable habits to deter them from their goal overriding all others: spiritual liberation.

One may derisively call them athletes of asceticism and renunciation. And to many modern, Westernized Indians they are an abomination, an embarrassing blot on their mainstream culture. But it should come as little surprise that many other people see them as powerful magicians who can be asked for advice and help on achieving mastery of their own lives and on expelling impediments from their own worlds. The yogic meditation schools might not go as far as the Aghoris, but they do put the main focus on self-discipline and concentration. Because as we recall Krishna saying in the Bhagavad Gita, thoughts are like wild horses we should rein in. So the point of this is that we should exercise control over our own habits of perception and thinking and learn to see the world through different eyes.

For example, asking your opponent for a favor can reduce enmity and rejection. As behavioral research and cognitive psychology have shown, such positive behavior toward another leads to a fundamental change in his or her previously critical or hostile attitude. This is also known as the Benjamin Franklin effect. The American natural philosopher, inventor, journalist, thinker, and politician Benjamin Franklin wrote in his memoirs about how he once dealt with an adversary who behind his back was relentlessly making him look bad in front of others and on top of that ultimately tried to prevent his re-election to the book and reading club Franklin himself had originally founded and up to then led. (Incidentally this book group was the first of its kind.)

Franklin, for whom the club represented a very important material livelihood, had the idea one day to send his opponent a friendly letter in which he asked to borrow a copy of a particular book he needed for some research. As the request was formulated in such a polite and friendly fashion, his adversary could hardly extricate himself from the wish Franklin had expressed and had the book delivered. One week later, Franklin sent the book back with a friendly letter of thanks. In the aftermath, these two fighting cocks became closer; in fact, an intimate lifelong friendship then developed between them.

Behavioral psychologists interpret the events as follows: after Franklin's opponent had done him a favor—and he did so quite politely in order not to show any weakness himself—he was faced with a problem of cognitive dissonance. On the one hand, he was Franklin's declared enemy. On the other hand, when he lent the book, he had been useful to him and had behaved toward him more like a friend or at least someone sympathetic. Thus he then ended up bringing his attitude toward Franklin into line with his behavior toward him and developed a sympathetic attitude for his adversary in order to resolve this dissonance.

The conclusion drawn from this story via behavioral psychology is as follows: It is in no way exclusively the case that we first of all form an opinion of someone (that is an opponent/a bad person/a rival) and *then* treat them accordingly. In fact, the exact opposite is the case. Our own behavior is "rationally" underpinned retrospectively by adjusting the attitude we have toward the other person!

For sure, Franklin's example omits any explanation as to why his opponent turned against him in the first place. In this respect the story has only partially been told, but all the same it provides us with an early case study of a psychological and cognitive process that since then has been as good as proven by way of scientific research. As neurology has demonstrated with the help of MRI scans, cognitive dissonance (e.g., "I don't like the guy, but I will still do him a favor") produces a conflict in the brain evidenced by the radically different blood flow in its corresponding regions that is ultimately detrimental to overall thinking activity. To compensate for this diminishment, or more precisely to end it, a value adjustment follows. In our example: "I can hardly have done a favor voluntarily for a guy I don't like. So in some way I must actually like him." This gets rid of the dissonance. The verdict on the other person adjusts itself according to the behavior towards him. If you can take the lead over your opponent in this way, to some extent you have already won half the battle.

Conversely this means that you should pay attention to whether you are susceptible to activating your own gratification center in the absence of other objective gratifications; for example, by desperately trying to find something good in unpromising situations or ones that bring you no benefit or are even harmful in order to "rationalize" them cognitively or emotionally back to yourself. Such reactions are actually irrational and can make you an easy target for others— it's precisely this form of adjustment that makes possible the exploitation of unpaid interns or voluntary workers and activists. In exactly the same way, soldiers and also suicide bombers are conditioned to overestimate themselves as heroes just like the followers of psycho-cults are forced into formulating their self-definition as enlightened, redeemed, or elite in some way. Thus open the floodgates to a complete letting go of reality.

Soul: Spiritual Malnutrition and How to Nurse the Spirit Back to Health, Not at Least Through Sober Self-Knowledge

The declaration that man does not live by bread alone originated in the New Testament but unfortunately has degenerated since then into a platitude. (The statement's accuracy, however, remains unchanged.) One may define the spiritual as one wants. It can be understood in purely religious or metaphysical ways, as religions and spiritual schools do. It can be grasped as a gateway to transcendence and the road toward it with a higher intelligence, though materialists, skeptics, or atheists may not agree, as it requires too many assumptions contrary to their beliefs. However, this does not necessarily need to be the case. Indeed, one can also look at the spiritual as an interlacing of its two subsets, body and mind, as a term describing the interplay between the two. Thus the "spiritual" can be understood as actually quite worldly and materially-based, free from any postulated supernatural transcendence.

The body craves periods of eating, resting, and recuperation as well as balanced movement and achievement recall. The mind needs food of a sort to keep itself occupied with intellectual stimulation and challenges, like conversation. As such, neither can the soul manage without genuine long-term support and sustenance. For a long time, support of this kind was offered exclusively by religions, often operating hand-in-hand with philosophy. Whether there really is such a thing as *Homo religiosus* as was claimed for centuries or in reality it might only be our brains' uneasiness when we have to interact with a world without any clear objectives, the sense of *futility* brings about an unacceptable deficiency in quality of life for many people. People who are happy to be called seekers by spiritual schools and religions are the embodiment of the need to do more with life than just serve a metabolism and satisfy some social ambition through the accumulation of material goods and status symbols.

Put your own spiritual convictions to the test. What do you believe in? What not? What meaning does the transcendent have for your life and why? (Or why not?) Can you answer the three classical gnostic questions for yourself with certainty: *Who am I? Where do I come from? Where am I going?* Reflect on how you deal with uncertainty both generally and in specific cases.

It is always a good idea as well to obtain precise knowledge about what other people believe or don't believe, what they might hold as true or untrue. The ongoing discourse on Islam in the West for example is characterized more than anything by a high degree of ignorance about Islam. But this holds true for both sides. Not only Christians and Jews but also atheists and agnostics understand very little about

Islam, generally speaking. There are also a great number of Muslims who barely have any detailed knowledge of their own religion, even when on a purely external basis they make a point of following the rituals and dietary proscriptions customary to their particular ethnic group and family and observe the designated holidays. In this respect, they are no different from the vast majority of those who still officially call themselves Christians but who at best know their holy book, the Bible, from a few extracts if not from mere hearsay. Sometimes it's precisely their agnostic opponents who in debates prove themselves to be much better grounded in the Bible even if they may not have access to the experiential religious dimension that is in fact freely available to the believer. Basically, it's a mistake to assume that belonging to a particular religion necessarily means that its doctrines penetrate into your own life anything more than superficially. Jews who barely know their Torah, Christians ignorant of their Bible, and Muslims unfamiliar with their Koran—this is the rule and by no means the exception.

Get engaged with as many religions as you can. Read their sacred texts: the Bible/Torah, the Koran, the Vedas, the Avesta, the Tao Te Ching (or in its more contemporary transliteration: Daodejing), the Buddhist sutras, the Confucian analects, the Book of Mormon, the Corpus Hermeticum, and so on.

We also recommend an engagement with the great philosophers, from the early Pre-Socratics through Socrates, Plato, Aristotle, and the medieval scholastics, the Renaissance and Enlightenment thinkers, on into the nineteenth century (Kierkegaard, Schopenhauer, Nietzsche, Marx, Haeckel, just to name a few) and further on to Existential philosophy (Heidegger, Sartre, Camus, by way of a few examples) and today's Postmodernism (Derrida, Foucault, Lyotard, Baudrillard, and others).

The best thing you can do initially is to engage with good introductions to their respective movements and themes. Study of the original texts without precise knowledge about their specific historical and cultural environments, the circumstances around their formulation and their variants can be difficult and at times downright misleading. For example, very few of the religious texts now appear before us today in their original forms. It's more often the case that they have undergone significant editorial changes and translations over the course of centuries and millennia. Secondary texts upon spiritual themes can also be extremely illuminating. The spectrum of these ranges from the confessions of St. Augustine via the confessions of Aleister Crowley to Yogananda's autobiography, to name a few representative titles.

Even though religious and mystical texts often treat states of rapture (that is, ecstasy) as their subject matter and the zealots in particular among their followers seem to be interested in hardly anything else, it's always preferable from a spiritual point of view to investigate them with a truly benevolent but not uncritical sobriety. Spiritual and religious statements cannot withstand such scrutiny because they exempt themselves from every critical examination and demand an uncritical submission to their postulations. Thus do they have about as much in common with genuine spirituality as the law and order outcry of far right movements have to do with actual, verifiable justice and the rule of law.

We should also critically consider all the fundamentalist currents that insist upon a literal interpretation of their particular canons of sacred scriptures without taking into account that every interpretation must out of necessity run through the filter of our present-day capability for verification, ending up correspondingly colored, if not fallible.

If you yourself tend toward wanting to bring the most complex questions and issues to as swift as possible conclusions via simple and undifferentiated answers and decisions, you should work on developing a somewhat broader (and in turn more sober) perspective on things. Everything else makes you vulnerable, whether you run the risk of becoming a victim of a sectarian Pied Piper or bloodying your nose by being argumentative, rhetorical, or even physical in debates and disputes with people who think differently. Insecure souls are particularly easy to manipulate by those who are skilled at dispensing self-confidence and unshakability, even if these qualities might often only form a very thin and easily penetrated façade.

Usually the real problem is that we are often the last to notice this in ourselves because our own bias and ego obstruct it. So our own misjudgments and mistakes are much more likely to be picked up by other critical observers and in the worst case used against us as well. By contrast, a well-informed, knowledgeable, and universal spirituality that hasn't taken on board any kind of world redemption ideologies through stupidity, ignorance, or fanaticism is always the more effective and powerful attitude of mind. That said, it also shouldn't fall into the grip of the impulse to rebuke unfamiliar/unconventional experiences and ways of thinking with arrogance and contempt in ways unchecked and prejudiced. So, just as in the Eastern context of enlightenment, it makes absolutely no difference whether and how you achieve it, spiritual realizations or truths can also get by quite happily without the murderous clamor of rival interpretations and their fanatical followers who are often only motivated by an absoluteness most brutal.

When you broaden your own spiritual knowledge and your personal experiences, consolidate them and in the truest sense of the word make them *livable*, you will question things with an open mind. Then you won't run any more risk of limiting your spiritual development through narrow-minded cowardice either. Ultimately, there is a reason why most of the wisdom teachings in human history have always recommended a state of composure and inner balance; it creates just the right state of being so a person won't get mixed up in the excited rush and aggression of cravings, fears, and passing fads. Such a stage of development is quite rightly described as *wisdom*.

It would not be proper to define wisdom as a noncommittal indifference to the world or leave it to those who want to turn it into hellishness while claiming that they only want to attain paradise. It's much more to do with creating a resolute spiritual *militancy* whose aim is not pulling the wool over anyone's eyes nor ignoring at the same time its own limitations and shortcomings.

Protocols
PROTOCOL CHAPTER 4–1
00:00–03:00 (180') *Phase 1*: Forest Walk 1
    (Centralizing your effort)
03:00–04:00 (60') *Phase 2*: Report

Explanations
Forest Walk 1 (Centralizing your effort). Follow a previously determined, tried, and tested woodland path at nighttime at a subjectively normal pace. At the same time, determine a (likewise subjective) reference value of 100 percent speed as well as 100 percent downward pressure (through the soles of the feet). After one-third of the total distance, reduce the walking speed to half (50 percent), and after the second third, reduce it again to 33 percent of the original walking pace. In parallel with that, also reduce the downward pressure to 50 percent and 33 percent, respectively.

It is admissible to illuminate your path occasionally and for a short period of time using a flashlight or something similar to avoid accidents, but this should be kept to the bare minimum and only used where really necessary.

Protocol Chapter 4-2

00.00–01.20 (80') *Phase 1*: Lying down

01.20–01.44 (24') *Phase 2*: Orienting yourself by your avoidance direction

01.44–02.00 (16') *Phase 3*: Note taking while walking around

02.00–02.17 (17') *Phase 4*: Lying down

02.17–03.00 (43') *Phase 5*: Systematic pressure point change

03.00–03.10 (10') *Phase 6*: Note taking while walking around

03.10–03.30 (20') *Phase 7*: Lying down

03.30–04.30 (60') *Phase 8*: Report

Explanations

Lying down. On your back (if necessary slightly skewed to the right), outwardly motionless, alert.

Orienting yourself by your avoidance direction. In the lying down position, determine your current overall body direction (e.g., the situation as determined by gravity) and immediately just on the impulse level, meaning without making any outward movement, turn in the other direction. If this is successful, then head in the currently opposing direction on the impulse level, and so on.

Note taking while walking around. For this protocol, you abandon your original position and work while standing or walking. You can walk up and down the room, or visit the toilet, etc. This helps with the production of additional self-alignment possibilities once you have returned to your lying down position.

In addition to that, you can use the time to make written notes, draw sketches, etc., which you can draw upon for hints at the end of the overall summing up in your reporting session.

Systematic pressure point change
While lying down, define five points on the body:

Right heel
Left heel
Right shoulder
Left shoulder
The middle of the back of your head

Over the course of the protocol, place your attention first upon pressure point 1 (right heel). This body point is to be determined precisely. Once this has happened (or your attention loosens or you find it starts wandering), change it over to pressure point 2 (left heel). Do the same thing here until the pressure point has been either precisely determined or your attention lets go or wanders. Then direct your attention toward pressure point 3 (right shoulder) and continue proceeding accordingly. Pressure point 4 (left shoulder) follows, and then pressure point 5, (the middle of the back of your head). Once you have done all you can at pressure point 5 direct your attention back towards pressure point 1, where the cycle begins anew.

Note: It is important to make sure that when determining the pressure points you don't treat them imaginatively (be it as an image or abstractly in your mind), but as tangible objects, which you can define with your senses!

PROTOCOL CHAPTER 4–3

00.00–02.00 (120') *Phase 1*: Lying down

02.00–02.15 (15') *Phase 2*: Note taking while walking around

02.15–03.30 (75') *Phase 3*: Marking your boundaries L

03.30–03.50 (20') *Phase 4*: Note taking while walking around

03.50–04.35 (45') *Phase 5*: Lying down

04.35–05.35 (60') *Phase 6*: Report

Explanations

Lying down. On your back (if necessary slightly skewed to the right), outwardly motionless, alert.

Note taking while walking around. For this protocol, you abandon your original position and work while standing or walking. You can walk up and down the room, or visit the toilet, etc. This helps with the production of additional self-alignment possibilities once you have returned to your lying down position.

In addition to that, you can use the time to make written notes, draw sketches, etc., which you can draw upon for hints at the end of the overall summing up in your reporting session.

Marking your boundaries L. A precise assessment takes place in the lying down position, of where the "alien" and "home" begin and continue on. While doing it, you begin at first with the body. The relevant areas are then also extended, as the case may be. In the note taking and reporting phases, the results are then documented in a schematic and graphic sketch.

PROTOCOL CHAPTER 4–4

00.00–00.50 (50') *Phase 1:* Lying down

00.50–01.45(55') *Phase 2:* Marking your boundaries S

01.45–02.00 (15') *Phase 3:* Note taking while walking around

02.00–02.20 (20') *Phase 4:* Lying down

02.20–02.50 (30') *Phase 5:* Systematic pressure point change

02.50–03.00 (10') *Phase 6:* Lying down

03.00–04.00 (60') *Phase 7:* Report

Explanations

Lying down. On your back (if necessary slightly skewed to the right), outwardly motionless, alert.

Marking your boundaries S. A precise assessment takes place in the lying down position, of where the "alien" and "home" begin and continue on. While doing it, you begin at first with the body. The relevant areas are then also extended, as the case may be. In the note taking and reporting phases, the results are then documented in a schematic and graphic sketch.

Note taking while walking around. For this protocol, you abandon your original position and work while standing or walking. You can walk up and down the room, or visit the toilet, etc. This helps with the production of additional self-alignment possibilities once you have returned to your lying down position.

In addition to that, you can use the time to make written notes, draw sketches, etc., which you can draw upon for hints at the end of the overall summing up in your reporting session.

Systematic pressure point change
While lying down, define five points on the body:

> *Right heel*
> *Left heel*
> *Right shoulder*
> *Left shoulder*
> *The middle of the back of your head*

Over the course of the protocol, place your attention first upon pressure point 1 (right heel). This body point is to be determined precisely. Once this has happened (or your attention loosens or you find it starts wandering), change it over to pressure point 2 (left heel). Do the same thing here, until the pressure point has either been precisely determined and narrowed down or your attention lets go or wanders. Then direct your attention towards pressure point 3 (right shoulder) and continue proceeding accordingly. Pressure point 4 (left shoulder) follows, and then pressure point 5 (the middle of the back of your head). Once you have done all you can at pressure point 5, direct your attention back towards pressure point 1, and the cycle begins anew.

Note: It is important to make sure that when determining the pressure points you don't treat them imaginatively (be it as an image or abstractly in your mind), but as tangible objects, which you can define with your senses!

5

YOU AND OTHERS

What the Expression
"No Man Is an Island" Really Means

No man is an Island, entire of itself; every man is a piece of the Continent, a part of the main; if a Clod be washed away by the Sea, Europe is the less, as well as if a Promontory were, as well as if a Manor of thy friend's or of thine own were; any man's death diminishes me, because I am involved in Mankind; And therefore never send to know for whom the bell tolls; It tolls for thee. —John Donne: *Devotions Upon Emergent Occasions* from 1624, Meditation XVII

This famous quotation from John Donne could not be more relevant. In a culture like ours, so committed to individualism that really hasn't evolved much beyond an overall aversion to all forms of dependence upon outside agencies, we might have a tendency to become accustomed to overestimating the limits of our freedom and self-sufficiency. Snappy sayings like "There's nothing I can't do" or "After me, the deluge" naturally only reinforce a fundamental misunderstanding because *egoism and self-centeredness have nothing to do with individualism!*

We cannot stress it here often enough: Not being aware of our limitations and weaknesses makes us open to challenges and easy targets for all kinds of manipulation. And holding ourselves to be self-sufficient and self-determined is one of the worst misconceptions. We would not have emerged out of nothingness nor would we have survived up to this day if we had not been steadfastly supported and encouraged by other people. It begins with our biological parents and spans our siblings and playmates, the collective experience of school and vocational training, as far as dating, starting a family and being locked into working life. It is said with good reason "it takes a village to raise a child."

In addition to this, each one of us, whether we accept it or not, is part of a community whose development and ways of functioning have a determined say in our lives. Take this one obvious example: Even if you might have no interest in politics, for better or for worse you are subject to its effects. Whether we are happy with it right now or we get stomach pains at the mere thought of it, we are subject to the decisions made by powers beyond our control. We might find then that the spectrum reaches from social interest groups and personal cliques as far as loftier determining factors like war, peace, the economic situation or the currently prevailing cultural norms such as morals and ethics. Even the Christian hermits in the Middle Ages were not exempt from this. There are numerous accounts in which they complain about being constantly afflicted even in the remote wildernesses by pilgrims and supplicants who begged for blessings from them or asked for them to intercede with God and the saints. Even then there was no trace of real solitude or tranquility; many of these good souls, people who really were striving for holiness and a state free from sin (in the Christian sense) lost their composure as a result and became hostile to their unwanted devout visitors, driving them away immediately with vulgar abuse.

A person is a social being from birth and remains one until death. We can certainly opt for isolation, but isolation does not have the slightest connection with genuine independence and self-sufficiency. The situation is made worse by the clear fact that we don't engage with most social interactions in a conscious way. From the point of view of self-protection, this means that we have to find some kind of clarity if we don't want to remain at constant risk of falling under the control of others, without even being aware of it. This will probably be especially surprising for most people when it comes to looking at the subject of motoric function.

Body: The Social, the Antisocial, and Yes, Even the Asocial Bodily Self-Alignment

In the course of this basic training, we have already covered the motoric and gravity. Here now we must start on *social motoric*. We understand by this the motoric self-direction with regard to other bio-organizations. In this text we will restrict ourselves to the examination of human beings. Of course social motoric also happens between people and animals but this is not the focus of our present engagement. Without resorting to the all-too-complicated theoretical considerations and description of abstract processes, we will formulate it in one simple maxim: *Each person aligns themselves upon every other person situated in their field of perception.*

What does "alignment" mean in this context? To express it in a somewhat pointed way, everyone—when it comes to their technique for self-alignment—relies upon someone else as long as this person can be found within their field of perception. So an individual moves in such a way that would have to end in a collision with the other if followed consistently. As a rule, though, it remains the case that by an inner alignment of the body, the outward manifestation of an actual impact or collision only follows in exceptional circumstances. To the untrained eye this inner movement will stay mostly hidden, even to the participants themselves. It does not unfold in a linear pattern; in fact, it involves a kind of inner vacillation, back and forth in the truest sense of the word. In the unremitting efforts of the body to withstand the pull of gravity upon the vertical (the downward), these secondary internal movements preventing collisions with external bio-organizations take place as an operational equalization.

The previously mentioned inner styles of Asian martial arts all strive for control over the internal regulation of bodily movement. That's also from where they take their name. Unlike the "outer" style where it's all about muscle building, increasing the reaction rate, hardening up and reinforcing the outer tissues, improving physical fitness and stamina, and so on, the inner styles are dedicated primarily to happenings within the body. Behind this stands the early recognition that the controlled alignment of your own inner movements can have an effect on your opponent exceeding in terms of efficiency what might be achieved using purely external techniques. The extent to which the teachers and trainers in the numerous martial arts studios specializing in the inner style actually do justice to these requirements all the time are another matter and cannot be discussed here further.

Since internal alignment takes place almost exclusively without any reflection (even unconsciously), you have to first bring it within the reach of your own will. The only prerequisite is your willingness to develop a high degree of attentiveness. You can effect this most easily through the ongoing observation of your own dynamic and its inner workings. It's best that you stipulate certain times for this observation at least initially. You don't have to sacrifice any of your free time or withdraw from the outside world to do this by any means. You can also do it while waiting at the bus stop, stuck in rush-hour traffic, brushing your teeth, or at the doctor's waiting to be called.

Let's take a very simple example, and you can apply the basic principles to all other operations of this kind: You're sitting at the table. There's a glass of water in front of you. You reach for the glass and lift it up to your mouth to drink. Then you put it back down again. Stop! Now you do the same movement once again, but you watch as closely as possible what going on inside you in a motoric sense, meaning with regard to the technicalities of movement. How does your body weight shift when you lift your arm? When you are stretching and when you are gripping the glass? Meanwhile, what is your back doing? The opposite shoulder? Did you move your foot even ever so slightly? Which one? How exactly? Did you move both? In what way, exactly? When did you open your lips? Did this take place only when the glass reached your mouth, or a little earlier? How much earlier, exactly? What happens when you swallow? What do your feet do? What do your abdominal muscles do? What about your neck?

Ascertain purely and simply what is going on inside you without judging anything as right or wrong. As a matter of fact, you can't make a mistake! Register as much as you possibly can from the overall movement process. Also try hard at all times to take a bearing on this observing and keep doing it without inwardly taking up any kind of position on it or evaluating the process.

Once you have carried out the glass of water visualization, you can apportion this kind of motoric self-observation in the future across the whole daily spectrum of movements you make. Then you won't need to keep carrying out the movement over and over again, either. For example, the next time you press the elevator button with your index finger, you will activate your inner observer at the same time. That on its own might be enough. There's no need to forgo your chat with your colleagues on the commute or block out their remarks because you are playing the absent-minded professor. What you're doing can't be described as distraction—it is a broadening of your perception capability.

Once you have managed this exercise for one or two weeks during which time you can maybe put in a daily quota of around ten to fifteen observation phases, you can then move on to observing your social motoric behavior in relation to other people. For this you don't need to do anything but observe your inner movements while remaining aware of the other people in your immediate surroundings while you talk to them, follow them (on the sidewalk perhaps or on the office floor), and dodge past them (for example in the pedestrian underpass or the queue for the ticket office).

First of all, pay close attention to your eyes. How exactly do they move when you watch another person who doesn't notice? What about when you speak to them? When they are just coming up to you? When you swerve around them while walking? When you go up to them and talk to them?

Now expand your self-observation. Do you change your body posture when you quickly scrutinize the other person without them registering any of it or being supposed to register it? When a colleague accosts you suddenly? Your boss? Your partner? When you come across two police officers while they are covering their beat? At the post office counter? When you are picking up the change they have given you at the ticket office? Are there differences between these social motoric encounters, and if so what are they? How do you carry yourself when you are on the phone with a colleague? With your child? With the boss? With the tax official who wants to talk to you about your returns? With your grandmother who's hard of hearing?

You can extend this across every area of your life, wherever you have anything to do with people: jogging in the park, lifting weights at the gym, at the riding club, in the swimming pool, at a restaurant or the theater, in a club or going for a walk in the woods. The opportunities are legion. Even if you are confined to bed or to a wheelchair, you can observe your social motoric encounters attentively as much or as little as you want. And here too you should not make any judgment or be on the lookout for what might be right or wrong.

You should also practice this for one to two weeks, perhaps ten to fifteen times a day, and whenever the opportunity presents. (You can't say for sure that you will come into contact with any one person on a daily basis.)

In the third and final phase of your observation of social motoric, you will become more proactive. Let's revisit the example of the glass of water on the table. Do the control movement again: Hold the glass, raise it to your lips, take a swallow, and put it down again. Now try picking up the glass and putting it to your lips *without* exerting any finger pressure. Be careful, you mustn't let it fall, or you will get everything soaking wet!

Impossible? Picking up a weight without exerting any pressure? Yes, that's how it is for as long as you don't have proper control over your inner movement. This though is exactly how you can develop it.

To do this, it's best to define a personal subjective scale of effort. The first time you did it, you held the glass of water with a *subjective* effort amount of 100 percent, lifted it to your mouth, and then put it down again. You can determine that quite simply and in an impressionistic way. Now try to carry out the same procedure with a *subjective* expenditure of effort of only 50 percent. Even if—according to your own observation—this might not actually work, try next time with a *subjective* expenditure of effort of 33 percent and one more time at a *subjective* level of 25.

Is that not ridiculous? Aren't you just convincing yourself that you have control over your motor skills when you really don't? Not at all! The key word in the exercise is "try." It should be nothing short of a basic rule: Even if you don't hold firm to it for all time, you keep failing with your intention. And anyway, what does *subjective* mean? It's purely arbitrary, isn't it? Well yes, it is that too! But at least it's *your* arbitrariness, and we are definitely not talking about the myth of objectivity either. What simply matters is that *you* make a serious effort to do justice to your tasks without losing sight of the desired objective in the process.

Those people who are used to collecting gold stars or brownie points for hard work, medals and trophies for finishing first, and clearly measurable success will perhaps initially find this difficult. At first glance, this practice seems completely unfamiliar, ineffectual, and artificial. But you will actually be able to grasp this way of proceeding as independent of any objective. Precisely this grasp itself will ensure that you can effectively escape the oppression and manipulation of others. Only a little patience is required.

Now you can transpose this experience into the continued management of your social motoric behavior. Starting now, you must in turn give up creating a control movement level for determining your subjective 100 percent because it really will seem a bit too conspicuous when you go up to a colleague twice one time straight after the other when they are supposed to know nothing at all about it. That said, you could do this perfectly easily with a practice partner who is just as interested as you in developing a better grasp on their social motoric. Continuing the example, go up to your colleague to talk to her but meanwhile also try to reduce the effort you put into your movement by half. "Reduced effort" does not mean moving more slowly! In the end it's all about the inner, not the outer, movement. How you undertake it is up to you. There are no tricks or rules for this that another person could pass on to you, but it's a good idea to keep making observations while you are carrying out the actual activity. However, you should unequivocally place your focus upon minimizing the expenditure of your social motoric. Should your powers of observation in the heat of the moment sometimes become less precise and detailed or even completely forgotten about, that's not such a big deal—just don't make a habit of it.

You will probably find out that a way of moving that minimizes expenditure as described above is much more satisfying than what you thought of before as your entirely normal personal self-modulation. It's certainly not forbidden to extend this form of inner modulation out to all your motoric encounters, not just the social ones, as long as it feels right to you and you bring the required application to it. We intentionally make no promises. It's always best to collect your own experiences instead of relying upon someone else's flowery testimonies.

Mind: Why There's No Point in "Trying to Understand" Someone Else—and What on the Other Hand Works Much Better

In popular psychology, you are often challenged to try to understand other people. By doing this you are not just nurturing an understanding for an opponent you might possibly come into conflict with but also stating that you will thus gain better insight into their intentions and then they won't be able to surprise you anymore. That may sound all well and good, but it is utter wishful thinking.

It isn't cynical to think that the vast majority of people don't even understand *themselves* let alone other people, to say nothing of strangers. For this reason almost above all others, *know thyself* was always the core demand of all the world's wisdom schools throughout history. More than anything, what this means is that one must abstract from oneself and one's own ideas to understand better the behavior of others and especially an enemy or opponent. If in your opinion all your opponents are motivated by envy only because envy is an especially detestable quality to you, you might overlook a completely different motive like, greed or fear of failure, for example. During the course of an escalation in the conflict, these can lead to entirely different kinds of behaviors and strategies, some you might only find out about once it's too late. So it is extremely difficult to objectify the complex processes in another unfamiliar psyche and to make accurate predictions about them. For that reason, such an effort is an utter waste of time without exception, more or less. Granted, if you know the person concerned very well and let's say you are aware of their patterns of reacting, strengths and weaknesses of character, and goals in life, it might at times seem different. Even then, for the most part, the prognosis remains a matter of luck.

It takes a great deal less effort and most of all it's more efficient by far to take the opposite approach and look into what pressure the other person is under. Incidentally, to do this we don't necessarily have to be dealing with an enemy. The same goes for friends, relations, colleagues, teammates, and passing acquaintances as well.

What kind of pressure might be meant? In this context, we mean everything that pushes people to carry out certain actions, and in extreme cases can even force them to do things they would most likely decline without being under that kind of influence. In this sense, there is perhaps also a "pressure" on you when you get up in the morning you only give way to because your job or family obligations require you to do so. The fear of being overlooked in the next round of promotions at work can manifest as pressure, which can lead, for example, to servile behavior or scheming and disloyal actions.

A police officer inspecting your vehicle at a roadside check is under pressure to behave according to the dictates of the legal system. However, he or she must also obey the orders of their superiors, like the one to carry out the roadside check at just that place and in just that same period of time. That officer must also proceed in a proscribed manner to issue a ticket or produce a warrant if need be, to provide a report on the entire proceedings, to submit this later on to the authorities, and so on. So here we see several kinds of pressure all at work at the same time determining that officer's actions and indirectly yours as well, because you must comply with the roadside check.

The nurse on night duty can determine her actions with as little autonomy as the doorman at the entrance to the club, the conductor in the train's carriage, the customs officer at the barrier, the radio announcer at the news desk, the plane's captain taxiing on the runway, and the lawyer during a court hearing. We are all under some sort of pressure that still determines our behavior, even if we decide to ignore it or even intentionally violate certain instructions and laws.

When you have to deal with an adversary at work or in a social group, in court or in a bar fight, don't waste any effort on trying in some ephemeral way to understand them. Strive instead to ascertain and get a handle on the pressure that other person is under. Is your colleague maybe only being that servile or scheming because he or she is afraid of being passed over in the next round of promotions? Perhaps you have heard that the person is under threat of prosecution for hit and run with potentially dire consequences under criminal law. Do you know that he or she has completely botched some operational issue and fears that this could now come to the surface and jeopardize their career trajectory?

More than anything else, try hard not to do one thing: *guess.* Constructing any fanciful grounds for making conjectures without any proven factual basis or contrived shots in the dark where you settle for a later explanation is only projection on your part, getting you nowhere. Always only proceed from verified facts. Sure, there will be a lot you won't know, and in other places you might have been completely misinformed. There might also be things that were perfectly unambiguous yesterday but have changed dramatically in the meantime without you noticing it. In order to protect yourself against this, you have just the one means available—summon up the greatest possible effort to keep yourself comprehensively informed. It's all you can do.

If you come out with an amateurish "I want to speak with your superior immediately" at the traffic control like a scolding fishwife, you will have then set in motion a defensive routine with your opponent that promises to do you more harm than good. Traffic officers are used to that sort of thing and they have been thoroughly well schooled in how to deal with it. That's why they won't be intimidated by it either. If, on the other hand, you pose the question "Would you please let me know the name of your officer in charge?" quietly, collectedly, and naturally in business-like and courteous tone, you can draw out a quiet different mood that from your point of view is usually more positive. You won't be able to pull your neck from the noose if you have actually committed an uncontestable misdemeanor, but simply using the technical term "officer in charge" in place of the vague "superior" signals to your opponent that he or she might be skating on thin ice and that greater caution is called for. And why? You, even without explicitly saying a single word about it, have stirred up the impression that you are better informed about police hierarchies than the average motorist, so the officer then must assume that you could cause him or her pretty major headaches (pressure!) in the event of any perceived misconduct on their part. Whatever happens, experience shows that the officer will treat you much more considerately from now on. However, as I have said already, should you have caused a serious accident, you will not be protected from punishment.

By the way, the unsophisticated "Of course, Officer; I know you have to do your duty" only rarely brings about the desired result. With overt subservience and an affectation of understanding that also happen to be the routine experience of every traffic officer, you will instead bring about the opposite of what you hoped to achieve. The reason is this: such an approach doesn't put the other person under control of their own pressure; it merely reveals your own. And it surely can't be hard for you to imagine which situation your opponent finds more compelling.

If you can detect what sort of pressure the other person is working under, opportunities to turn the situation to your own benefit begin to appear. Aren't you grateful when someone else offers to relieve some of your burden? It's that way for everyone. Strictly speaking it's also a matter of a certain way of handling the pressure. Whether physical or emotional in nature, it is experienced consciously (as well as unconsciously) as pressure, a thing people are only too happy to be rid of. Where relief is promised, something pleasant and desirable becomes possible, and that awakens sympathy. Out of this we can say that a person is naturally always more interested in the pressure they are under than in that of others. So try your best to isolate what sort of "relief dividend" comes into the equation for you when you assume leadership over the other, rather than grant them rulership over you. That may sound banal, but in many cases it's surprisingly simple to carry out. Consider the courteous and polite expression of a request rather than a blustering *demand*. Pick up a pencil that had rolled onto the floor and pass it back to the person behind the desk, even before you have formally introduced yourself to them—such an act is frankly trivial and definitely unspectacular but under the circumstances it may still qualify for a very effective approach with which you can save yourself stress and annoyance that would only manifest once again as even greater pressure.

What might at first look like a small and very modest beginning can develop into an extremely powerful weapon when consistently pushed forward. In more complex scenarios in which a great deal of money, power, or influence might be at stake, you probably won't get very far with such small gestures. And yet the basic principle always remains the same: the other person is under some kind of pressure that he or she is constantly trying to evade. As you recognize this pressure and—at best unexpressed, so as subtly and as unobtrusively as possible—convey the impression that you don't want to contribute to it but can in places perhaps reduce some of it or even remove it completely, you will achieve a great deal more than you would with every stubborn insistence on your legal rights or demands for satisfaction. Of course, do not give up on what is rightfully yours. But for just that reason the pressure the other person is under should interest you at least as much as your own, since correctly handling this reveals the way to relieving your own burden.

It should be left up to you to develop your own approaches when dealing with social commitments and expectations.

Soul: The Meditative Determination of Human Networks and How You Can Avail Yourself of It

Jack Kerouac describes a Buddhist practice in his novel *The Dharma Bums* where you put yourself into a meditation posture, close your eyes, and imagine someone you know. When you can see or feel that person internally, say the words silently to yourself: "[That person's name], equally empty, equally deserving of love, equally becoming Buddha." According to Buddhist interpretation, we are all on the way to Buddhahood whether we know it or not. Proceed in the same manner with the next acquaintance, friend, or family member and continue the meditation until you've included everyone you know.

The notion of "becoming a Buddha" will not be meaningful to everyone, and the particular term isn't even absolutely necessary—this emphatically recommended meditation practice is not difficult to adapt your own world-view. Your formula could for example go: "… equally empty, equally deserving of love, equally the way to self-realization." And should you be bothered by the term "self-realization," replace it with whatever suits you more, like "happiness" or "freedom," for example.

If you have a very large circle of acquaintances, you can also divide the practice up across several sittings perhaps to include your relatives first, then your friends, and finally your colleagues and other people in your life.

In Buddhism this practice serves to develop and accentuate compassion for other people. You might find that welcome or you might not. We are mainly concerned with increasing our awareness of our social network and defying the current superstitious beliefs that we are just autonomous and metaphorically speaking, islands. With the inclusion of the word "equally," we are of course holding up the mirror to ourselves. So *you too* are vain and empty, just like everyone else—although that does not mean you have to stay that way.

So think of this practice as a kind of sober contextualizing and keep performing it at greater intervals, perhaps on an annual basis. It really can't do any harm to remain mindful of the very finely spun web that binds us all together positively as well as negatively.

Protocols
PROTOCOL CHAPTER 5–1
00.00–01.20 (80') *Phase 1*: Lying down
01.20–04.20 (180') *Phase 2*: Impulsing in circular
    phases 5/5
04.20–05.40 (80') *Phase 3*: Lying down
05.40–06.40 (60') *Phase 4*: Report

Explanations

Lying down. On your back (if necessary slightly skewed to the right), outwardly motionless, alert.

Impulsing in circular phases. An alternation between lying down and/or sleeping, and activities done while standing up, divided into phases. The latter can be performed using any activities you like, and the digits following indicate the value in minutes of the particular phases (e.g., 5/5 is five minutes sleep/five minutes standing up, and so on).

Tip: As you can easily lose perspective when you perform this technique over a longer period, it is recommended you keep a checklist to document the individual phases you have completed.

PROTOCOL CHAPTER 5–2

00.00–01.30 (90') *Phase 1*: Lying down

01.30–02.15 (45') *Phase 2*: Technical sleep

02.15–02.30 (15') *Phase 3*: Note taking while walking around

02.30–03.35 (65') *Phase 4*: Technical sleep

03.35–03.45 (10') *Phase 5*: Note taking while walking around

03.45–05.45 (120') *Phase 6*: Lying down

05.45–06.45 (60') *Phase 7*: Report

Explanations

Lying down. On your back (if necessary slightly skewed to the right), outwardly motionless, alert.

Technical sleep. The aim here is to cross over directly into the sleep state without a transitional stage ("a gradual darkening" etc.). It is to be expected that this (initially) won't be successful, but if so one should continue to make an unbroken effort to get closer to it.

Note taking while walking around. For this protocol, you abandon your original position and work while standing or walking. You can walk up and down the room, or visit the toilet, etc. This helps with the production of additional self-alignment possibilities once you have returned to your lying down position.

In addition to that, you can use the time to make written notes, draw sketches, etc., which you can draw upon for hints at the end of the overall summing up in your reporting session.

PROTOCOL CHAPTER 5–3

00.00–02.00 (120') *Phase 1*: Lying down

02.00–03.15 (75') *Phase 2*: Marking your boundaries L

03.15–03.30 (15') *Phase 3*: Note taking while walking around

03.30–04.45 (75') *Phase 4*: Lying down

04.45–05.30 (45') *Phase 5*: Note taking while walking around

05.30–06.45 (75') *Phase 6:* Orienting yourself by your avoidance direction

06.45–07.05 (20') *Phase 7:* Note taking while walking around

07.05–07.50 (45') *Phase 8:* Marking your boundaries S (S IS FOR STANDING)

07.50–08.35 (45') *Phase 9:* Lying down

08.35–09.35 (60') *Phase 10:* Reporting

Explanations

Lying down. On your back (if necessary slightly skewed to the right), outwardly motionless, alert.

Marking your boundaries L. A precise assessment takes place in the lying-down position, of where the "alien" and "home" begin and continue on. While doing it, begin at first with the body. The relevant areas are then also extended, as the case may be. In the note taking and reporting phases, the results are then documented in a schematic and graphic sketch.

Note taking while walking around. For this protocol, you abandon your original position and work while standing or walking. You can walk up and down the room, or visit the toilet, etc. This helps with the production of additional self-alignment possibilities once you have returned to your lying down position.

In addition to that, you can use the time to make written notes, draw sketches etc., which you can draw upon for hints at the end of the overall summing up in your reporting session.

Orienting yourself by your avoidance direction. In the lying down position, determine your current overall body direction (e.g., the situation as determined by gravity) and immediately just on the impulse level, meaning without making any outward movement, turn in the other direction. If this is successful, then take a bearing once again upon the currently opposing direction on the impulse level, and so on.

Marking your boundaries S. A precise assessment takes place in the lying down position, of where the "alien" and "home" begin and continue on. While doing it, you begin at first with the body. The relevant areas are then also extended, as the case may be. In the note taking and reporting phases, the results are then documented in a schematic and graphic sketch.

Protocol Chapter 5–4

00.00–01.15 (75') *Phase 1*: Lying down

01.15–01.30 (15') *Phase 2*: Note taking while walking around

01.30–02.45 (75') *Phase 3*: Impulsing in circular phases 5/5

02.45–03.00 (15') *Phase 4*: Note taking while walking around

03.00–03.45 (45') *Phase 5*: Lying down

03.45–04.45 (60') *Phase 6*: Reporting

Explanations

Lying down. On your back (if necessary slightly skewed to the right), outwardly motionless, alert.

Note taking while walking around. For this protocol, you abandon your original position and work while standing or walking. You can walk up and down the room, or visit the toilet, etc. This helps with the production of additional self-alignment possibilities once you have returned to your lying down position.

In addition to that, you can use the time to make written notes, draw sketches, etc., which you can draw upon for hints at the end of the overall summing up in your reporting session.

Impulsing in circular phases. An alternation between lying down and/or sleeping, and activities done while standing up, divided into phases. The latter can be performed using any activities you like, and the digits following indicate the value in minutes of the particular phases (5/5 is five minutes sleep/five minutes standing up, etc.).

Tip: As you can easily lose perspective when you perform this technique over a longer period, it is recommended that you keep a checklist to document the individual phases you have completed.

6

VAMPIRES, WEREWOLVES, AND ASTRAL PARASITES

How You Protect Yourself from Being Sucked Dry

It's hard to dispute the fact that life first and foremost takes the form of a contest and struggle for resources. And naturally this is not just the case in the animal kingdom. Human civilization and culture can be understood as a set of rules full of processes and ordering systems that aim to curb the wild beast in every human, to regulate their aggression and in this way to facilitate the creation of halfway stable communities, which are more conducive to humanity's survival as a species than the battle of one person against the other. You can have a first-rate debate about the success or failure of this undertaking, especially since it has assumed different forms over the course of history. In the end you can't fail to notice either that all these efforts by human nature collectively as well as individually were able to set curbs on it only to a very limited extent.

Resources are always scarce, whether it's clean drinking water, game to be hunted, fertile and arable land, or all those raw materials we needs for the creation of tools, weapons, clothing, shelter, and transportation. Not yet has there been a time in which humanity could simply lean back and be cossetted and cared for by nature. Everything we need to survive has to be wrung out of the earth using blood, sweat, and tears. And it's a characteristic of every larcenous act that it takes the resources of others wherever seen as necessary and feasible.

It is an idea that also applies to human interaction in so-called civilized forms of society. As networked and dependent on others as human beings are, they must not only be concerned with their own care and maintenance, but also must—in the interest of their very survival—fend off, prevent, and incapacitate others' attacks.

One of myths' essential functions is explaining the world in a narrative way. They dress up life experiences and events in a narrative fashion, shaping them into a form both informative and entertaining, making them mediators above all. The tales, legends, and fables of vampires and werewolves all convey the mythical dim and shadowy dangers humanity sees itself exposed to during its earthly sojourn. They are found in many cultures and take on the most varied forms. Therefore, it often requires a very thorough and persistent analysis to uncover the universal core message.

The Transylvanian version of the vampire legend should probably be most familiar in Europe, and it seems at first glance to have little in common with Babylonian demonology, the Seth-myths of ancient Egypt, or the fabled djinns of pre-Islamic Arabic culture. And yet we find on closer inspection that they actually do have so much in common—above all, danger embodied in living entities. On top of that, the question is not of sober/rational scientific lab reports but of narratives that have undergone so much embellishment and reforming over the course of their centuries or even millennia of transmission. In this way the respective original versions are often so bowdlerized, garbled, and reworded to the point of being utterly unrecognizable.

When we speak today of vampires and werewolves, very few people in our latitudes probably believe in the genuine existence of such beings. They are all the more familiar to us because of the entertainment industry with its horror films and novels. In recent decades, this inventory of terrifying creatures has—sometimes jokingly, sometimes meant seriously—embraced the concept of zombies originating out of the Voodoo cult in Haiti as well as the Juju of Benin and its neighboring West African states. With its eclectic body of teachings, theosophy made the concept of astral parasites popular in the nineteenth century, or at least popular in the occult world and the later esotericism movement.

Like all stories, myths are to be understood primarily as figurative and not literal. Accordingly, we adapt them in everyday life to the currently prevailing paradigm. Thus we understand terms like "vampire" or "werewolf" at first psychologically. Everyone is familiar with this: get-togethers and conversations with people after which you feel shattered and completely drained although there definitely weren't any obvious incidents that might explain why. Many people don't really even need to be ostensibly down in the dumps or talking about any depressing issues for you to feel dejected and downright overwhelmed after only a brief conversation. Often, all that's needed is the mere presence or a simple thought relating to the relevant person to unleash these destructive processes. For this reason, it's not difficult to see the person concerned as a vampire, who is sucking the blood—that is, your vitality—out of you, without giving anything back in return.

Experiences with "werewolves," meaning with people who change all at once into nothing short of murderous beasts and wreak untold damage only then to assume again their friendly and even placid personalities as if nothing had happened, are less commonplace. Criminology and psychology have been dealing with such "wolf people" for a long time now; usually they are found in the category of serial killers. But a serious bloodbath doesn't always have to be the aftermath for such werewolf associations to present themselves. People with strongly marked manic-depressive personalities or borderline personality disorders can supply comparable fear and terror to their surroundings through behavior.

However you might explain these phenomena, the bottom line is that these sorts of behaviors and personalities can make life hell if you don't know how to effectively protect yourself against them. And protection can definitely be set up as long as you take the appropriate measures.

Body: The Way that Bodies Occupy Space and Disarming People from a Distance

It might sound like a truism, but the safest way of protecting yourself from the clutches of vampire types is to just not let them anywhere near you in the first place. In most cases, that's enough. Such people seek out the proximity of others, to put it another way. In their (often completely unconscious) struggle to benefit from the vitality of others, they are utterly dependent upon gaining actual access to their victims. Even if they don't sink their fangs into your jugular vein like the vampires of legend, they have to get close to you in the first place to suck you dry. Here as in all other matters, a person usually follows the path of least resistance. You will be quickly left alone as soon as the vampire has established—once again usually completely unconsciously—that you are stubbornly out of reach.

More than anything else, this process is based upon motoric adjustment. As has already been explained, bio-organizations always tend to take a motoric bearing on each other for as long as they can be found in each other's field of perception. This collision-stabilizing movement remains mostly a purely internal one not actually expressed outwardly. Obviously, that does not make it any the less real, and this is the precise point where you can take action to shield yourself from becoming a vampire's victim.

The next time you encounter a vampire like this or suddenly become suspicious that you are dealing with one, you should do the following:

First, reduce your own inner collision movement in the direction of the relevant person to zero. To do this, you must for a start naturally be aware of theirs. It is recommended that you read back over the dedicated sections in the earlier chapters on the subject of bodily self-alignment if need be. You will continue to execute your general interior movement adjustments; in fact, you have to execute them, as discussed already, so you don't collapse to the ground. But this time rein in your "falling toward the other," even if you are looking at, talking to, and even touching that person.

Now restore that inner falling movement towards a collision with the other person once more, *but only up to half-distance.* So if the other person is one meter away from you, of course you can steer your inner movement in their direction, but let it end at half a meter away as if their body already began at that point and offered its collision point there for you to take your bearings. You can observe it in the reverse as well. It's as if you shift your own body in terms of inner steering (purely motorically) on to that point half a meter away. This is only inwardly, of course, not to be implemented outwardly. It might happen that your widening the distance visibly irritates the other person. Their movements can sometimes then become erratic or downright spastic; in any case, to the extent to which you have successfully aligned yourself as described he or she will want to change their distance from you. But always retain your inner self-alignment at half distance. If the other person gives way or moves away a bit, just expand your own orientation accordingly. If he or she comes closer to you, then reduce your alignment distance by the corresponding 50 percent. Coming into contact with one another during this whole time is still possible. The question—at least from the point of view of your subjective perception—is of reducing pressure for you and not them. To train yourself in this, you are best off experimenting with a practice partner, if you have one on hand.

No matter what now happens motorically, stay at half distance with an iron will. Usually this will have no outwardly recognizable dramatic consequences. It is still crucial, though, that you really limit yourself to bodily self-alignment and don't try anything like "helping" the procedure along a bit using facial expressions, eye movements, or even the spoken word in any shape or form. It's much more important that your actions regarding that other person are inscrutable, even if his or her fine motor perception is likely to be signaling something quite different to them. Using this procedure, you create a kind of cognitive dissonance in which your body modulation and bearing signal something that stands at complete odds with your facial expression, eye movement, and whatever you might be sending out acoustically.

But beware, this particular explanation serves only as an illustration and it reduces the whole process to just a few factors. The process we describe here is actually much more complex, but discussing it in all its detail would take too long. It is preferable that you take note of your own experiences if you want to reach some reliable conclusions. Of course, this won't work if you only do it on paper; it has to be carried out under real-world conditions.

Taking firm control of your own subtle motoric skills—especially the social motoric as covered in the previous chapter—is one of the foundations of conducting a successful conversation, even ahead of any rhetoric or skill at constructing an argument. Whoever manages to start leading the other in as much as he or she wrests control of the motoric-oriented collision points from the other will retain the upper hand in conversation, even where social hierarchies like for example boss/employee, ruler/subject, kidnapper/hostage, and similar continue to dominate the overall situation instead of letting themselves fall under the other's spell.

You can also use this approach in other contexts where out-and-out vampire or werewolf natures are not involved. Then you can also experiment with various steering distances. What effect will you achieve with half the distance? What about three-quarters? One-quarter the distance? What does the other person do when you oscillate back and forth in short succession between two different distances, say 50 percent and 25 percent? What about when you let the collision point you are projecting oscillate for a period of time initially very quickly, then all of a sudden very slowly, and very quickly again?

It should be mentioned here that you should avoid trying these experiments with people who are especially close to you since it can result in a loss of trust; the person concerned might not adequately be able to put into words or know how to substantiate. Ultimately, it is of no benefit to you if you set off a vague disquiet among your loved ones even unintentionally via the suspicion that they are being manipulated and controlled from the outside. It's much more preferable to seek out people for this with whom you are not so keen on maintaining a close connection.

You can also combine this procedure with your own outward movement. You should try it out when you are next alone and undisturbed. For example, you might reach externally for the door handle when you want to open the door but inwardly you only steer half the distance toward it, and so on. What happens when you steer inwardly toward a point *behind* the closed door? Maybe you need to move a heavy cupboard. Steer on an experimental basis toward a point that lies quite a way *behind* the cupboard, perhaps even slightly set to one side of it. How does that change things compared with your normal pushing movement? When you want to lift weights in the gym or grab a full crate in the liquor store, do the same thing.

A variation between your inner and outer modulation will also lead to different experiences compared to the times when they both correspond to each other and merely overlap. You can determine for yourself which form of self-alignment offers the most ease of use and is thus the least wearing. From this you will also be able to draw many a useful lesson for your everyday way of living. You can optimize a great deal, avoiding unnecessary effort for you, thereby increasing your efficiency and reducing wear and tear at the same time. That should also eventually manifest itself in a significant enhancement to your quality of life.

Mind: The Foundations for Successful Negotiation

We have mentioned this already: By no stretch of the imagination does conducting a conversation consist of just rhetoric, reasoning technique, and discussion routines. Physical motoric behavior is always in play as well, as our communication is not restricted anyway to pure speech, requiring instead a number of varied signaling channels. Indeed we open up very few of them consciously. Facial expressions, facial movement, the impression of our eyes, gestures, bodily posture, speech characteristics, tone of voice, speech volume, but also our interior collision self-alignment all belong in this group. With it we broadcast information signals just as we receive and process the corresponding signals coming the other way from our interlocutors.

Many people have a problem lying convincingly. Why is that? They can construct the most convincing, plausible and refined cock and bull stories and yet people who only vaguely know them or sometimes even complete strangers can see through their maneuvers and in the worst cases unmask them publicly and cause them the embarrassment of exposure. The reason for this is often cited as "a lack of acting talent." But what does that really mean?

A closer look at the art of acting will help us here. Many of us have perhaps experienced it ourselves when we joined the school or local theater company. It is not enough to memorize the text for a role while maybe making a few appropriately held faces and adding in some reinforcing gestures. Good, compelling—yes, even brilliant—actors are one thing above all else: confident. This not only means that they appear sure of themselves and believe in themselves in their role. More than that, actors have a less convincing or talented effect when their delivery and movement, facial expressions, gestures, voice, and facial delivery do not match with each other. Confident actors, however, create overall plausibility. The text they are reciting thus represents only one quite important but by no means utterly crucial component.

When you are all brashness, bravura, and no substance in a conversation where you are performing or promoting something but your body posture is signaling to others that this is just a role being played, rehearsed, or something soullessly calculating and constructed, you will hardly convince anyone that you are genuine. On the contrary, we generally don't like it when people look to us like they are acting, because from our point of view it seems false and manipulative, which is indeed often the case. To identify play-acting like that for what it is, people can necessarily use only their own senses, but relying on them can often misfire. It's often no help against devious con artists and crooks who understand their craft as well as a sublime actor knows his or hers.

The question here is not about learning to lie better and more convincingly but of taking a firm grip on our countless signaling channels. Often enough the most banal everyday conversation will present us with a veritable combat zone. The "battle" can be about who is imposing their interests against the other person's, who has the final say over whose decisions should take precedence, or who knows how to take advantage of the other. This can often play out in the most banal everyday events even between lovers and long-term partners. The flakiness of the pastry, the strength of the coffee, or the positioning of the jam at the breakfast table suddenly become the material for a never-ending dispute of course fueled in reality by completely different things that usually remain unspoken. Even those people who continually claim that they don't mince their words and always say everything immediately as it comes to mind often also signal a great deal that is unspoken, no matter if they aren't really personally aware of it.

Thus the interpersonal conversation is often a sort of Trojan horse, a stratagem. Since we continue to experience these sorts of things over the course of our lives and would like to protect ourselves against them, we ourselves then suspect hidden messages or secret intentions in places where the other person has actually simply meant it straight and without any ulterior motive, just as it was put forward. Upset and a lack of confidence are the regular outcomes of such failed acts of speech.

Speech is silver, silence is golden is one of the platitudes of modern talk therapies, but it's been repeatedly shown to be inaccurate in everyday life. Indeed, you should add to it: *Listening is platinum.* Because a person can actually only speak successfully when not just letting the other talk but also registering what's being conveyed—and by that we don't just mean the acoustic material—with the greatest of attention. In this respect you can never proceed too meticulously! It is really not the same thing if the other person says "well, I think" or "well, I believe," or whether they say "all this rubbish" or "all this crap." It might be that this subjectively conveys the same thing more or less to you at first, but you should guard against projecting your own communication filter uncritically upon the other person in the conversation. Only when you are aware of exactly what your opponent is signaling to you can you also determine where you yourself should intervene to take the conversation in the direction in which you want it to go. And when you bear in mind what we have already determined along the theme of pressure and pressure structure when it comes to conducting a conversation, you might arrive very quickly at quite different and much more effective ways of speaking compared to how you have been operating up to now.

Of course it won't do us any harm to engage on an ongoing basis with rhetoric and logical thinking. Each of us is very susceptible to errors of thought on a day-to-day basis; they are often not so readily identifiable without the appropriate training. With every mistake in logic, we expose ourselves in an unwelcome fashion, and an adversary cunning enough will quickly work out how to exploit it. Conversely, being able to recognize errors in arguments and analyses can bless you with a major advantage over others. The same goes for many other discussion techniques as it surely does for the whole art of argumentation. Delve into the appropriate literature, certainly, but also be aware of the limitations of such material that doles out advice. There is hardly anything more laughable than a linguistically inept speaker who tries to simulate determination with a few choreographed and clumsily translated moves, such as the wooden raising and lowering of a clenched fist, when even the untrained eye notices immediately that the person is operating beyond their rhetorical means. Politics serves up hair-raising examples of this on a daily basis. Bad acting is really just hamming it up, and you will achieve no lasting success with ham acting. Sticking with the example of the clumsily wielded fist: If the rest of the body seems stiff and immobile while you are doing it because the movement itself is just based around the shoulder joints, then this gesture comes across not just as clumsy, but, even worse, insincere. Unfortunately, most rhetoric teachers don't carefully consider the motoric component of this process, although it is of paramount importance.

Listening is quite another matter. Quite irrespective of the content of what is being said, the other person is also conveying a great deal of information all the time about their basic relationship with you and the world in general. You should determine and classify this as precisely as possible.

Most people would rather talk about themselves than listen to the talk of another person. They are often only a short step away from delivering a pure soliloquy. Where needed, this can be induced with ease, although the result is not always the most edifying experience. It can sometimes happen that a person might have you in their pocket for three hours solid and talk the whole time without comma or period, not expecting any reaction whatsoever from you. Usually the occasional nod of the head or clearing of the throat will suffice on your part, a "hmm" or a "yes" to keep the other's flow of speech going. And at the end, the person will thank you for the "excellent conversation" and slink off! Now, in the worst-case scenario you'll have been thoroughly bored and yet as a result have learned somewhat more about the other than they of you. And should it ever come to a conflict between the two of you, the old police formula will apply of course: "Everything you say can and *will* be taken down and used in evidence against you." Obviously, you should not make the same mistake.

In front of the mirror, check out the ways in which you deliver certain phrases, statements, or whole speeches. (By the way, experienced politicians and their coaches do this on a regular basis.) Prepare a few set phrases in advance, ranging from everyday sayings like "Do you have a light?" "What time is it, please?" or "How do I get to the station?" to political statements such as "This foreign policy is a catastrophe!" "This politician has never up to this point shown any backbone!" "This kind of economic policy is exactly the right one at the present time!" and so on. In addition, prepare poems, longer theater pieces (the "To be or not to be" monologue from *Hamlet* is very popular), and whatever else you might come up with.

Our intention here is not to open an autodidactic theater school. For now, establish all the different ways in which you can recite a text. Pay attention to your enunciation, speed of talking, volume and emotional impression, to your facial expressions and gestures, to the play of your eyes and definitely to your overall bodily motoric. Now try it with some minor adjustments. How does it come across when you deliver the Hamlet monologue with one hand in your trouser pocket? With both hands stretched up towards the ceiling? With your index finger in your ear? With your left leg forward? With your head tilted slightly to one side? With raised eyebrows? With a deeply furrowed forehead? Standing on tiptoes? It's best if you make your own discoveries and establish what works best for you. As long as you are always ready to make corrections and compare your insights with your everyday experience so you can learn from it on an ongoing basis, this is and will remain a method that should deliver success.

Soul: Sigils, Mantras, and Mudras for Spiritual Protection (and also for Protecting Other Loved Ones)

You have learned all about sigil magic and been given instructions on the creation of an effective magical sigil of protection in basic training. The written verbal method introduced there should be perfectly sufficient, but I should mention now that there is also a mantra-based method of sigil magic that works with purely aural sigils. Because of their phonetic quality, they take on the character of mantras.

When we talk about mantras, we are usually talking about meaning-rich or meaning-free sound sequences originating from the spiritual cultures and traditions of the East. Mantras are regularly repeated during meditation or ritual to induce a state of spiritual trance and implant its assertion or active power into the soul. Even meaningless mantric syllables like *om, hram, hrim, hrum,* and similar count as transmitters of power that can be used to bring about certain specific effects. We can find comparable phenomena in the Kabbalah, ancient Egyptian and Greek magical papyri, as well as in the Gnostic literature of late antiquity.

A mantra that's also very well known in the West is the Tibetan *Om Mani Padme Hum*. It is usually translated somewhat strikingly, as "hail to the jewel in the lotus." In Tibetan Vajrayana Buddhism, however, it actually carries a great deal more meaning, but unfortunately we can't go into all the details here. There are also mantras in Christianity. Consider, for example, the *Kyrie eleison* of the Roman Catholic and Orthodox churches. In Islamic Sufism and its various dervish orders, there are often suras from the Koran or short devotional formulas like *La Ilaha Illallah* ("There is no god but God"). And so you find in all cultures these formalized sound sequences that embody a particular active power. These are also often recited in ritual chants, woven into oral and written stories and accounts, and used in sacred objects, pictures, and even ritual tattoos.

With the mantra method of sigil magic you will proceed in a quite similar manner to the word method. First, you formulate your statement of will but reduce it to just its consonants (here as well each letter is only used once). The vowels I, A, or O can now be randomly inserted. So you get a mantra, which can consist of one or several "words" that don't need to have any recognizable meaning in and of themselves.

To illustrate, let's reuse the statement of will from chapter 3. The statement, reduced once again to its consonants, appears as follows:

N, X, T, W, K, B, P, R, S, D, Y, M

Once you have added the vowels and moved the consonants around, you could get for example the following mantric sigil:

NAXO TOWAKI TIBOPA ROSODI YAMO

Or instead:

NIXOTAWI KOTABIPO RASO DAYOMA

You can create a sigil mantra for protection against particularly stubborn or malignant "vampire" or "werewolf" natures in your surroundings, for example. And by doing this you can also guarantee the protection of your loved ones.

This sigil mantra is activated by repetition as long and as monotonous as possible, during which you should forget once again the statement of will and its content as thoroughly as you can.

It is possible and in many cases even preferable to repeat the mantra for a limited period of time silently over and over to yourself, perhaps while out walking, waiting in line at the supermarket, on the plane, or wherever else the opportunity arises. There is no authoritative answer to the question of how often or how long this mantra has to be repeated; rely on your feelings and your intuition. Most importantly, as before, make sure that the mantra and its repetition (out loud or silent) is forgotten as soon as you stop doing it per the basic training for sigil magic.

Another highly effective approach to creating magical protection for yourself and others is constructing mudras. Mudras are potent gestures usually performed using the hands. Some have a certain meaning, others use subtle forces, and some even contain both. Gods, demons, saints, gurus, and other spiritual role models are often represented using carefully defined hand and finger positions. Mudras are also often used in the meditation practices of different schools of yoga. It is said of them that they symbolize, produce, or promote specific states and levels of awareness and knowledge.

More than anywhere else, you can find them used in Hindu and Buddhist temple dances, primarily in India, Thailand, and Sri Lanka as abstract representations of feelings or emotional states like joy, sorrow, anger, fear, courage, or doubt. In other Southeast Asian cultures as well, like those of Vietnam, Cambodia, and Burma, they form part of a traditional canon of symbols transmitted to the adept as statements through gesture and as such find their use in the dance-based presentation of historical or religious myths.

In their heavily corrupted form—meaning in popular superstitions—the traditional mudras are often understood to be magical gestures in each of which a particular mode of operation is assumed. In this way, the knowledge of their original function and mode of operation has largely been lost as happens so often in folk traditions. In its place a rigid dogmatic cataloging has taken over: Gesture 1 brings about fertility, gesture 2 creates wealth, and so on. The modification discloses nothing of the mudras' original formation or their possibilities for application.

Symbolic gestures are endemic to every world culture. Consider for example the folding of the hands in prayer that can be observed not just in Christianity but in the Shinto religion of Japan and in devotional practices in Taoist and Buddhist temples as well. And of course, gestures and gesticulations also play a large role in nonreligious fields. Greeting handshakes are widespread, and many know the meaning of Winston Churchill's victory sign and the Boris Becker fist-pump of the modern tennis-player. Even the yielding empty palm gesture as a sign of being unarmed and of peaceful intention is one of these.

Whatever happens, you shouldn't mistake these gestures for actual mudras, because these actually embody a specific motoric modulation that both represents and induces mental/spiritual states of mind. In addition, they can manifest as a kind of trigger switch for certain motoric states in a condensed form.

A simple and very lucid term for this we know from psychology and the practice of neuro-linguistic programming (NLP), is "anchoring," referring to the bodily memory that can be selectively activated through certain gestures and movements to memorize spiritual states and retrieve them when needed.

Take up a position again in front of a mirror. Try hard to produce a simmering strong emotion. You can pick joy but also anger, love as well as hatred, irritation as well as tranquility. Assume one single emotion and turn it up to maximum intensity. Now create a unique mudra that consists of one single finger gesture. For example, as a mudra of joy you could connect the tips on the thumb and middle finger of your left hand. Maintain this gesture while the emotion slowly subsides. During the entire process, observe yourself in the mirror.

Now try it with the next emotion, anger for example. Once again, work the emotion up into a crescendo, except that this time you will anchor it with another gesture, say, by holding the tip of your left thumb on the head of your little finger. Maintain this gesture until the emotion has completely evaporated again.

You can carry this exercise out any number of times and manufacture an extensive inventory of emotionally binding individual mudras, a kind of sign language of the soul. In the early days, you should awaken the corresponding emotion in yourself when the opportunity arises by activating the mudra. However, this should continue as a purely internal process not outwardly reflected in expansive gestures or facial expressions. In other words, make it as unobtrusive as possible. So for example, let joy or anger surge up only internally while you activate the mudra. Then finish making the mudra gesture, whereupon the emotion will straight away begin to subside.

Once you have practiced this for a while, you can also create mudras for your own protection to fend off hazards or exert influence over others. These gestures should always remain as unobtrusive as possible so that no one is able to keep pace with any of it. For example you can hide your hands in your jacket pocket or behind your back so that you can activate the particular mudra without being seen.

There are some indications that words originally acted as aural gestures that in a way were shifted up into the organs of speech in order to leave the hands free for other tasks, such as aiming a spear, raising an axe, or firing arrows, and the like. If this theory is indeed sound, it would mean that speech originally reflected the human inner motoric and even replaced it, at least partially. Austin Osman Spare seems to have been quite aware of this when he said that "sigils will flesh." And it seems very probable that the development of mudras also lies at the root of this phenomenon, especially as we know of them from Eastern spiritual practices.

Protocols

PROTOCOL CHAPTER 6–1

00.00–01.30 (90') *Phase 1*: Lying down

01.30–02.00 (30') *Phase 2*: Greater mudra

02.00–02.45 (45') *Phase 3*: Lying down

02.45–03.30 (45') *Phase 4*: Greater mudra

03.30–03.45 (15') *Phase 5*: Note taking while walking
    around

03.45–05.30 (105') *Phase 6*: Technical sleep
05.30–06.00 (30') *Phase 7*: Lying down
06.00–07.00 (60') *Phase 8*: Report

Explanations

Lying down. On your back (if necessary slightly skewed to the right), outwardly motionless, alert.

Greater mudra. In a sitting position, let your upper arms rest gently against your torso. Touch the fingertips of both hands (all ten fingers, i.e., including the thumbs) gently against each other, forming pairs. Then first of all reduce the pressure between the fingers of one pair, and next let it go completely, while still maintaining the contact between them. Eventually, carry out the same procedure with four fingertips, thus two further pairs, until at the end all the fingertips are still resting against each other but without expending any pressure.

Should the fingertips become separated from each other, start the greater mudra all over again.

Note: You should make sure that this does *not* become a matter of imagining (whether it's figurative or abstract/mental). Instead it should be a genuine bodily and sensation-based operation.

Note taking while walking around. For this protocol you abandon your original position and work while standing or walking. You can walk up and down the room, visit the toilet, etc. This helps with the production of additional self-alignment possibilities once you have returned to your lying down position.

In addition to that, you can also use the time to make written notes, draw sketches, or create other visual media you can draw upon for hints at the end of the overall summing up in your reporting session.

Technical sleep. The aim here is to cross over directly into the sleep state without a transitional stage (a gradual darkening, fading, etc.). It is to be expected that this won't be successful initially, but you should continue to make an unbroken effort to get closer to it.

Protocol Chapter 6–2

00.00–01.00 (60') *Phase 1*: Lying down

01.00–01.30 (30') *Phase 2*: Steering fingers

01.30–01.40 (10') *Phase 3*: Note taking while walking around

01.40–03.10 (90') *Phase 4*: Technical sleep

03.10–03.45 (35') *Phase 5*: Lying down

03.45–04.45 (60') *Phase 6*: Report

Explanations

Lying down. On your back (if necessary slightly skewed to the right), outwardly motionless, alert.

Steering fingers. Write by hand on an 8½ by 11-inch piece of paper for up to thirty minutes, eyes closed, on a theme of your own choosing.

Note taking while walking around. For this protocol, you abandon your original position and work while standing or walking. You can walk up and down the room, visit the toilet, etc. This helps with the production of additional self-alignment possibilities once you have returned to your lying down position.

In addition to that, you can use the time to make written notes, draw sketches, etc., which you can draw upon for hints at the end of the overall summing up in your reporting session.

Technical sleep. The aim here is to cross over directly into the sleep state without a transitional stage (gradual darkening, fading, etc.). It is to be expected that this won't be successful initially, but you should continue to make an unbroken effort to get closer to it.

Protocol Chapter 6–3

00.00–01.30 (90') *Phase 1*: Lying down

01.30–02.00 (30') *Phase 2*: Lesser mudra 1

02.00–02.15 (15') *Phase 3*: Note taking while walking around

02.15–03.00 (45') *Phase 4*: Lying down

03.00–03.10 (10') *Phase 5*: Orienting yourself by your avoidance direction

03.10–03.55 (45') *Phase 6*: Lesser mudra 2

03.55–04.20 (25') *Phase 7*: Note taking while walking around

04.20–04.40 (20') *Phase 8*: Lying down

04.40–05.40 (60') *Phase 9*: Report

Explanations

Lying down. On your back (if necessary slightly skewed to the right), outwardly motionless, alert.

Lesser mudra 1. In a sitting position, rest your upper arms against the sides of your body, and touch the tips of one pair of fingers (e.g., your index fingers) gently against each other. Then first of all reduce the pressure between the fingers, next let it go completely, *while still maintaining the contact between them.*

Should the fingertips become separated from each other, you must start the lesser mudra all over again.

Note: You should make sure that this does *not* become a matter of imagining (whether it's figurative or abstract/mental) but instead that it's a genuine bodily and sensation-based operation.

Lesser mudra number… See above. The numbers are there to indicate how many pairs of fingers to work with. With the number 2 that means two pairs (the index and ring fingers for example), with the number 3, three, and with the number 4 four pairs of fingers. No thumbs are used!

Note taking while walking around. For this protocol, you abandon your original position and work while standing or walking. You can walk up and down the room, or visit the toilet, etc. This helps with the production of additional self-alignment possibilities once you have returned to your lying down position.

In addition to that, you can use the time to make written notes, draw sketches, etc., which you can draw upon for hints at the end of the overall summing up in your reporting session.

Orienting yourself by your avoidance direction. In the lying down position, determine your current overall body direction (e.g., the situation as determined by gravity) and immediately just on the impulse level, meaning without making any outward movement, turn in the other direction. If this is successful, then take a bearing once again upon the currently opposing direction on the impulse level, and so on.

Protocol Chapter 6–4

00.00–01.00 (60') *Phase 1*: Lying down

01.00–01.10 (10') *Phase 2*: Flat walk 100%

01.10–01.20 (10') *Phase 3*: Flat walk 50%

01.20–01.30 (10') *Phase 4*: Flat walk 33%

01.30–01.40 (10') *Phase 5*: Flat walk 25%

01.40–02.10 (30') *Phase 6*: Note taking while walking around

02.10–02.50 (40') *Phase 7*: Lying down

02.50–03.50 (60') *Phase 8*: Report

Explanations

Lying down. On your back (if necessary slightly skewed to the right), outwardly motionless, alert.

Flat walk 100%. Cover a determined distance at a normal walking pace. This is to be carried out initially with a normal downward pressure of the soles of the feet, in order to determine the (subjective) reference value of 100% pressure expenditure.

Flat walk 50%. Like 1, but with half the downward pressure (50%) in comparison with the previously established reference value.

Flat walk 33%. Like 1, but with one-third the downward pressure (33%) in comparison with the previously established reference value.

You can proceed accordingly with further percentage figures. (So, 10% = 10 percent pressure expenditure, always in comparison to the previously established reference value, and so on.)

Tip: Take care to work *with* gravity instead of against it.

Note taking while walking around. For this protocol, you abandon your original position and work while standing or walking. You can walk up and down the room, or visit the toilet, etc. This helps with the production of additional self-alignment possibilities once you have returned to your lying down position.

In addition to that, you can use the time to make written notes, draw sketches, etc., which you can draw upon for hints at the end of the overall summing up in your reporting session.

7

SUCCESSFULLY ASSERTING YOUR OWN INTERESTS

Dominating Through Simulated Support

We spend a great deal of our lives asserting our own interests against those of others, aligning ours with theirs, or submitting to others' under constraint. Naturally, the latter is rarely the desired outcome and counts as one of the least pleasant experiences we might have. Already as children we learn that our plaintive "I want! I want! I want!" is normally dashed sooner or later upon the rocks of parental resistance. Playmates and teachers also place clear limits on the implementation of our desires. And yet that doesn't prevent us from pressing forward with the enforcement of our own interests.

Where we are dealing with other people, it often makes much more sense to determine first of all precisely *their* area of concern rather than wrack our own brains over how to enforce our own will as successfully as possible. The same goes here as it did with our studies of pressure structures, namely that the other always assumes a more important position than our own in as much as "important" here means quite literally "exerting weight" which usually assumes the form of pressure like weight and strain. So the next time you mean to tell someone that you would like to be considered as more important in some way, you should mull over more carefully what you are actually saying. Weight, burden, and pressure—none of this is good for you. "Importance" here is resistance and hindrance, attrition and hassle. For that reason you should also pay the closest attention to that person to protect yourself from them.

As experience teaches us, we often get much further in life when we use diplomacy and good negotiation skills rather than with surly and arrogant demands. In any case, that kind of bluster is usually only flaunted by those people who behind everything are very insecure, often also riven with anxiety. These sorts try to hide their insecurity through a feigned outer toughness and intransigence. Aggressiveness is generally a rather transparent maneuver that hardly ever works with opponents who have been seasoned in combat and are reasonably intelligent. As an anonymous cynic once said: "Diplomacy is sending someone to hell but in such a manner that they look forward to the journey."

It can actually happen though in a much more subtle way. In many martial arts schools the testimony of a venerable old master is quoted where he states without hesitation that the highest level of mastery does not consist of winning every battle but much more of taking care that the conflict or battle *doesn't even happen in the first place*. This is not an indicator of any battle-shy pacifism, however. The statement shouldn't be misunderstood either as the ultimate expression of a readiness to compromise. It's much more a matter of enforcing your own interests as effectively as possible so your opponent does not even manage to build up any worthwhile resistance against them. This means ultimately that you should take the other person under your control and prevent them from even attempting to impose their dominance over you.

Body: How to Carry Your Body for Dominance

In the conventional conception of the motoric facility, we generally equate weight and fighting power with dominance. This might have to do with the fact that when in doubt, our Stone Age brain continually depends upon primitive strategies of violence. The hunter who shoots the deer brings it down. In plenty of cases, the deer is only wounded and tries to flee. Then the hunter or the hunting party will bear down upon the deer in order to wrestle it to the ground. Only then can it be killed. The situation is similar in what is probably the oldest sporting discipline derived from direct combat: wrestling. In this sport, you must bring your opponent down to the canvas and apply your weight on them in order to make continued resistance and flight impossible.

It seems obvious that size and weight are decisive when it comes to the creation and pursuit of dominance and authority. In myths, heroes are often portrayed as muscle-bound giants. And even today we would have difficulty imagining a Hercules as someone small and weedy. Consider also the humorous maxim: "The fat can assert, but the thin must justify." For that reason, Asian martial arts mainly concern themselves with enabling the smaller, thinner, and more flexible types to triumph over the larger, more solid, and stronger ones. Dwarf versus giant—it's the old cross-cultural theme of David defeating Goliath. Therein lies the promise of these martial arts disciplines, which is reflected in many of their formative legends. In these myths, it's almost always only the old or the less powerful souls who prevail in conflicts against their larger, younger, and stronger opponents—*not* by simply resorting to the use of their body weight, as this wouldn't serve them much anyway against a physically superior opponent.

Here too we are dealing with the key to success through the mastery of social motoric. In this case, it seems to be somewhat more complicated; if you have followed the previously discussed reflections and recommendations, however, what we are now recommending should actually be very easy to implement in practice.

We have already addressed comprehensively the motoric collision point—how to detect it, how to project it, increase its range, withdraw it, and more. For the physical management of dominance, there is only one single proviso:

Always offer the other person the seemingly closest support point *without* ever honoring this promise.

We have established that concerning interior self-alignment with the collision point, it actually comes across as a maneuver to ease a burden; with its help we can pacify our ongoing conflict with the force of gravity. That person who doesn't want to come crashing down will support themselves against a tree, lamppost, the wall of a house, a walking stick, or even on another person. This support is for sure only a substitute method of handling it.

What we have up to now tagged a collision does not necessarily remove the need for conflict, but it should to an extent help to make the self-alignment against gravity less of an effort, even if on closer inspection it tends to remain an illusion. This process almost always plays out without any self-reflection and is therefore unconscious. For this reason, a true alleviation does not take place, if only because we can so readily look to a friend or a tabletop for support. However, the weight of our body remains the same, so we can't really talk about any objective facilitation in the sense of becoming lighter.

It's a part of the automization of the untutored human motoric always to steer towards the closest, or more precisely, the *next-closest-seeming* support point. This is not a linear movement; it is subject to variations and oscillations. This also has to be the case inevitably, because everything else leads to an over-steer, which will then result in an actual fall. To that extent, the support points in the vicinity which are in varying degrees available to people, exist in competition with each other. On the other hand, you can make use of this by setting your interior fine motoric orientation, so as to project your collision or support point upon the other until there's nothing else left available to them, than to keep steering toward it.

As we clarified already, you should not carry out the following experiments with people who are personally very close to you. The exception to this is of course your training partner. So use someone—as determined in the previous chapters—with whom you have advanced your collision point through *interior* modulation (thus not outwardly expressed), so that no external physical contact will take place. In this way, you are attentively following the motoric self-alignment of others as inconspicuously as possible. Does a change take place at all as a result of your projection of a support point? If so, what kind of change? Does the other person incline, perhaps to a microscopically small degree, toward your projected collision point? Or do they swerve aside from it? Do they steer toward you in the course of a subtle wavering process, then move away again? What's the reaction when you swing the collision point back and forth, letting it oscillate quickly?

At the start, you will have to comprehend the whole process in detail, before you can continue. Once you have succeeded, you can embark on the process at any time straight away and without any advance analysis. Do you "have" the person? Have they actually fixed their alignment on to your projected support point yet? If so, keep hold of this non-physical contact that of course only takes place on the external effects level, even if it produces demonstrable external effects. And now retract the projected support point a miniscule amount without releasing the contact in the process. Is the other person following you motorically? Then you've done it!

If this is not the case, keep trying. It may well be that you will only succeed on the hundredth, thousandth, maybe even ten thousandth attempt. This depends on the quality of your own modulation, and unfortunately there are no tricks or fail-safe rules that might help you shorten the process. The only true avenue to follow is your own ceaseless effort which should mainly be expressed in constant self-correction. But as has been mentioned: Once you have truly managed it the one single time, you will never again lose this ability.

Note here also the second part of our requirement, the so-called promise that never actually will be followed up on. When we spoke above about contact, we did not mean that one bodily weight should press against the other. For as soon as this happens, the law of physics holds sway, wherein the larger and heavier mass either supplants or places gravitational pressure upon the smaller and lighter one. In this case, it is of the greatest importance to maintain contact but not allow any build-up of pressure in the process. Therefore, when the other person takes a subtle motoric bearing upon your projected collision point and comes to rest on it, you should never offer them the desired static support. Instead, you relocate the promised support point negligibly, thus keeping him or her constantly on the move and ultimately taking the other person motorically under your control. Then you can also lead them wherever you want.

In many martial arts schools and forums, people tend to talk of so-called contactless techniques about which the most fantastic stories are often told. Granted, some of them may well be exaggerations, especially when you have to deal with some breeds of alleged masters who claim to have mastered these techniques but who also get out of actually providing proof of it with the help of a lot of mystical rumors. Others are quite capable of doing it on occasion and actually demonstrate this kind of thing, though usually in front of a small inner circle of intimates, and you have to gain access to that august elite in the first place. As a rule, it is not enough simply to make people aware of your appropriate interest. There are many legitimate reasons for this reticence we cannot explain here in any detail. Mostly it's just a matter of trust.

When you hear about someone—in a process that doesn't involve any physical contact and hence no bodily movement—catapulting an opponent across the hall or about another person without laying a finger upon a master standing motionless in the room even though they is not evading them in any recognizable way, then you can say for sure that something of this kind does actually exist. The explanations offered for this admittedly often range from the fantastical to the abstruse. Usually the concept of chi (something we have considered previously) must be pre-assumed mandatorily without the encumbent explanations actually providing any plausibility.

Other disciplines, like the previously mentioned Russian Systema, don't really bother at all with explanations but just rely on practical action. This might not be to everyone's liking; on the other hand, wiht Systema, you won't be hassled by some hair-raising speculation that insults your intelligence.

Mind: How You Can Direct a Conversation with Others Unnoticed

This section ended up being short. What we said above on how you hold your body will also find powerful expression in how you conduct a conversation. Should you have any doubts, you can readily try it out with seminars in rhetoric and argumentation as well as with training in logical thinking. There is absolutely nothing objectionable in that. However, you should not get yourself confused either when doing it. You will hardly ever be able to manufacture the same amount of that drawing-in technique we covered simply by substituting in slick rhetoric.

It's more important at this point to advise you that all this is in *no* way a matter of a form of imagination. Much more than that, we are discussing quite real and objectively verifiable effects we have credited sorcerers, witches, medicine men, and shamans with since ancient times. It may well be that in the course of human history actually only a few of the so designated above were truly able to produce such a powerful effect. The chance coming together of various phenomena possibly coupled with the ignorance and credulity of the watching audience; a serving of self-confident coolness, combined with the ability to submit to the whiff of mystery and to deviousness—on more than one occasion such a combination of conditions may have served to help a shaman or a miracle worker, a magician or a witch to undeserved fame. Perhaps it was only an infinitesimally small minority that actually developed these kinds of skills. But in contrast to the way that rationalization and scientific superstition want to pull the wool over our eyes, such phenomena are by no means to be banished into the realm of fables and legends, of fairy tales and tall stories.

You need to believe—nay, you shouldn't actually believe what's being presented here! Ideally, you will make your own discoveries. You should only be ready to devote a bit of time, effort, and patience to open-minded experimentation. No one who is being sincere can promise you success, just like a language course cannot offer any guarantee that you will at some point actually gain perfect mastery over a foreign language you are learning. This does not mean, however, that it is impossible. Sometimes it can even happen almost instantaneously, albeit on extremely rare occasions. As a rule, however, it requires quite some time expenditure and a continued persistence.

Soul: The Three Rituals of Self-Assertion

Here are three rituals that access elements of various magical traditions. The Lesser Banishing Ritual of the Pentagram originates in the hermetic tradition of ceremonial magic as it was revived in the nineteenth century by the order of the Golden Dawn. The IAO Protective Shield Ritual makes use of the old Gnostic IAO formula and offers a very simple and swiftly generated protection through inner centering. Finally, the Thanatos Ritual deals with the "mystical death" and adopts elements from Tibetan Chöd and the Mexican Santa Muerte cults.

Rituals are generally magical and invariably cultic procedures that pursue a particular purpose. This purpose could be the manufacture of a protective shield, the triggering of certain states of consciousness, the setting in motion of magical processes, or targeted contact with energies or entities to name but a few. Furthermore, what makes it a ritual is its repeated practice; it is not carried out merely once, as a rule. It takes place multiple times, frequently also on a regular basis. For example, in the religious sphere we know the Christian mass, the Jewish Sabbath celebration, the Islamic daily five prayers facing Mecca called the *ṣalāt*, in addition to countless other activities, such as the celebration of fairs and festival days, processions, pilgrimages, and so on. By definition, the term *ritual* should always be used in a neutral—non-judgmental—sense unlike what the representatives of certain religions are regrettably so fond of doing because from their perspective the word is loaded, linked to the reprehensible activities of heretics and Pagans or mere superstitious magical practices. The word actually derives from the Latin *ritus*, by which a firmly structured act of worship is designated a solemn religious custom. In everyday speech, we use the term in a mostly pejorative sense for a strongly formalized, more or less meaningless action, such as when we speak of an "election campaign ritual."

It's up to you which of the rituals proposed here you want to start with; the listed order is not compulsory. The meaning, object, and purpose of the individual rituals will each be discussed in the explanations.

The text that follows has been taken (with minor changes appropriate to our present subject matter) from my 2011 book, *Money Magic: Mastering Prosperity in Its True Element* (Llewellyn Publications).

THE LESSER BANISHING RITUAL OF THE PENTAGRAM

The pentagram (also known as pentacle) is an ancient symbol that can be found in Stone Age rock carvings. It is familiar to almost all the peoples and cultures of the earth. In the Western/ Occidental magical tradition, it stands for the five classical elements: earth, water, fire, air and spirit (ether). At the same time, it symbolizes a standing human being with spread legs and arms stretched out at the sides. Each of the elements is allocated to the points of the star, as shown in Figure 5.

In order to make the later notes clearer, there now follows the complete technical description of the Lesser Banishing Ritual of the Pentagram itself. You will find the explanations attached.

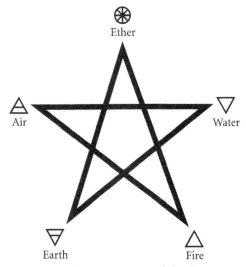

Figure 5: The pentagram and the elements

The ritual is carried out while standing, facing east to start. The gestures are performed using the right or the left hand, and the direction of movement for drawing the pentagram itself remains the same for right- and left-handed people. If applicable, you can work with a magical dagger or athame or your outstretched index and middle fingers with thumbs just alongside them.

The Kabbalistic Cross

Using your fingers or the dagger, draw power down from above onto the top of your forehead. Touch it and in doing so vibrate with power the term:

ATEH ("Thine is")

Now touch the center of your chest and in doing so vibrate with power:

MALKUTH ("the Kingdom")

Now touch your right shoulder and in doing so vibrate with power:

VE GEBURAH ("and the Power")

Now touch your left shoulder and in doing so vibrate with power:

VE GEDULAH ("and the Glory")

Now cross your arms upon your chest and with the palms of your hands laid on your shoulders vibrate with power:

LE OLAM ("forever and ever")

Now place your hands together in front of your forehead, draw them down to in front of your chest and vibrate with power:

AMEN ("so be it")

The Drawing of the Pentagrams and of the Circle
Now draw the first pentagram, all the time facing east. Consult Figure 6 for the direction of movement.

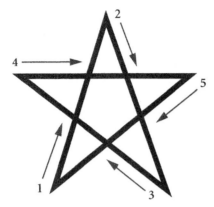

Figure 6: The direction of movement for the
Lesser Banishing Ritual of the Pentagram

Next, breathe in and draw your hand back toward your
chest. Then make an abrupt pointing movement with your
fingers or the dagger towards the center of the pentagram
you have drawn, and while doing so vibrate with power the
Hebrew name of God:

YHVH (Yeh-ho-vah or Yod-Heh-Vau-Heh)

Now step around the circle keeping your hand outstretched like before, until you come to a stop facing south.
Repeat the drawing of the pentagram. Point toward its center
again and while doing so vibrate with power:

ADNI (Ah-do-nai)

With your hand still outstretched, walk around the circle until you come to a stop facing west. Repeat there the

drawing of the pentagram, point toward its center, and while doing so vibrate with power:

EHIH (Eh-hey-yeh)

With your hand still outstretched, walk around the circle until you come to a stop facing north. Repeat the drawing of the pentagram, point toward its center, and while doing so vibrate with power:

AGLA (Ah-g-lah)

With your hand still outstretched, walk around the rest of the circle until you are facing east again. The circle is now closed, reaching from pentagram center to pentagram center.

Invocation of the Archangels

Looking to the east, stretch your arms out to the side and at the same time visualize yourself as an oversized black cross with, at the crossing point in front, a large red rose blooming brightly. Once this visualization has been set up, visualize with the vibration of the archangel's name its larger than life form, in the shape of a human being. Their locations are specified in the text.

While doing so, speak the Hebrew names with a powerful vibration:

Before me RAPHAEL
Behind me GABRIEL

To my right MICHAEL
To my left AURIEL
Around me flame the pentagrams,
Within me shines the six-rayed star.

Figure 7: The hexagram (the Star of David, the six-rayed star)

The shining six-rayed star is also called the hexagram and is visualized in the color gold (see Figure 7).

The Kabbalistic Cross
Proceed once more as above under point 1.

Dismissal Formula (at the end of the complete ritual)
A dismissal formula is not set in stone. In its specific detail, it might also be oriented according to the content of the complete ritual that went before it. So please find here only a suggestion, one which in practice is used frequently:

"With this I release every being and energy that has been banished by this ritual. Draw away in freedom. May peace reign between you and me!"

NOTES AND EXPLANATIONS ON THE
LESSER BANISHING RITUAL OF THE PENTAGRAM
On forming the Kabbalistic Cross

When forming the Kabbalistic Cross, the hand draws a beam of white light through the crown of the head and into the body, then through the solar plexus (the "plexus of the sun") down toward the feet, and finally from the right to the left shoulder until the whole body is irradiated by a cross of light. In the Christian tradition, the spoken formula (though of course not normally in its Hebrew version) is known as the supplement to the Lord's Prayer. Despite the Judeo-Christian symbolism used here, no involvement in the Judaic or Christian religion is needed for the successful deployment of the Lesser Banishing Ritual of the Pentagram. In fact, it is also used on a regular basis by Neo-Pagans, atheists, and followers of other religions oriented toward the hermetic-classical tradition of magic.

On drawing the pentagram and the circles

By "drawing" what is really meant is tracing the symbols. You can see for yourself the exact direction of movement in Figure 6. This drawing takes place near the body and the total height of the pentagram should be around one meter. It's recommended you tailor the movements to the rhythm of your breathing: ascending line—breathe in; descending line—breathe out; horizontal line—hold your breath.

While you are marking out the pentagrams and the circle, visualize or imagine that colored energy (whitish blue, silver, or red) is streaming out of your moving hand so that the pentagrams and the circle are gleaming in your inner space. (It can take many months and even years of practice until you can actually observe them with your physical eyes. This does not mean, however, that the symbols are only effective when they appear—they always were. The tradition here describes a "magical perception" that for most people requires appropriate training.)

The vibration of the names of God should be done so powerfully that they cause the whole body to oscillate. In the older texts they say that "the walls of the Temple should shake," and here the "temple" refers to the body. This is not a question of loudness! This also entails the names of God resounding in your acoustic imagination in whatever direction they are spoken in "up to the end of the universe" and in this way penetrating all that is.

Depending on the external conditions, the formulas of the Lesser Banishing Ritual of the Pentagram can be intoned only in a very quiet or an almost silent way where necessary. What is crucial here is, as mentioned, not the acoustic volume but moreso the intensity with which it occurs. The goal of intoning the formulas in Hebrew is the induction of a magical trance, which can work according to one's experience significantly more quickly and intensely than the English translation as determined by the sound quality of the Hebrew words.

On the Invocation of the Angels

Like the names of God, the names of the archangels should be vibrated in a long, extended way. Here too the requirement is to shake those "temple walls."

The figures of the individual archangels, who simultaneously embody the function of the essential elements, are based on the following iconography.

Raphael stands in the east and is ruler of the air element. He wears a yellow robe and carries a rod as well as a jar of ointment. During the invocation, imagine a light wind from the east blowing on your face.

Gabriel stands in the west. He is the ruler of the element of water. He wears a blue robe and carries a chalice, while he stands in a clear, flowing waterfall. During the invocation, imagine the water is rippling behind you and feel its moisture.

Michael (also said as "Mikael") stands in the south and is the ruler of fire. He wears a shining red robe and holds a flaming sword in his hands. In the south, that is, to your right, imagine the heat of fire during the invocation.

Auriel (also written and spoken as "Uriel") stands in the north and is ruler of the earth element. He wears an earth-colored robe (brown and olive green tones) and holds a sheaf of corn ears in his arms. He stands in the middle of a wheat field, perhaps on a pentacle as well. During the invocation imagine in the north, to your left, the solidity of earth.

As already mentioned, the hexagram (hovering above the head of the magician) is imagined as gold. Its size is not fixed; bear in mind that in group ritual, one should agree on this beforehand for simplicity's sake.

You need to make sure that you are aware of all these elements of the Lesser Banishing Ritual of the Pentagram simultaneously! You are aware of the pentagrams and the cross; you also hear the vibrating names of God; you yourself are at the same time a great black cross with a red rose; and you also see/feel/are conscious of the archangels and the powers of the elements.

We can see that in the case of this part-ritual that comes across so inconspicuously, we are actually dealing with a veritable encyclopedia of hermetic/magical symbolism. At the same time, it places great demands upon your powers of imagination and visualization. But in a different way to what we are in general familiar with as children of an industrial and achievement society, the matter here is not of attaining an end point which is perfection from which all the components of the Lesser Banishing Ritual of the Pentagram are performed in absolute completeness. In fact, the term "perfection" really means that any further improvement is blocked off—so as a result it's something dead and empty of soul. Yet it's something to strive for, so it's always like a utopia, as a never truly attainable and exhaustible but desirable ideal condition. Symbolically it means: It always goes on. The process never reaches its end. And in it you can also see a formula for immortality.

What was said at the beginning still applies: don't get discouraged when you make mistakes. Symbols and images are fluid and flexible. That's what constitutes their strengths.

On the Kabbalistic Cross
What was written above also applies to the renewed drawing of the Kabbalistic Cross.

On the dismissal and thanksgiving formula
The concluding dismissal and thanksgiving formula fulfills two functions at the same time. Firstly, it represents a kind of subtle "hygiene measure" because now all the entities (mental models of magic), powers and energies (energy models), disturbing thoughts, associations and feelings (psychological models), or unwanted junk in the data stream (information models) attracted by the ceremony are released.

On the other hand, it signals a return to the everyday life state, and where necessary, dissolves things. This at the very least will stop you from being burdened with factors outside the ceremonial magic events that are only valid in the world of magical symbols. Expressed in very simple terms, you could also say that this will be an effective prevention against possession and madness.

THE IAO PROTECTIVE SHIELD RITUAL
The IAO Protective Shield is an energizing and self-protecting ritual that makes use of the vowel sequence I—A—O, which played an important role in late antiquity Gnosticism.

The ritual describes the specific use of each individual vowel as a "formula": thus the I-formula, the A-formula, and the O-formula.

In its operative process, the IAO Protective Shield Ritual is similar to the Kabbalistic Cross used in the Lesser Banishing Ritual of the Pentagram but considerably less complex and in some respects even more effective. Above all, in ceremonial magic it serves to harden the aura of the magician, thus enabling an optimal level of magical protection.

To begin with, the IAO Formula should always be performed while standing (see Figure 8). Once you have practiced it a few times, you might also make use of it in other positions.

The I Formula

Stand upright with your feet close together, preferably facing east. With your eyes closed or half closed, intone the vowel sound *I* (pronounced *ee* as in "bee") in a long, drawn-out way:

"Iiiiiiiiiiiiiiiiiiiiihhhhhhhh"

At the same time, imagine a vertical beam of light, that descends from above and enters through the top of your head. It then continues vertically through the middle of your body to the bottom, where it disappears into the ground. (This stream of light has, however, no defined direction of flow. With time it actually feels like it flows simultaneously from above to below and from below to above, usually in rhythm with your breath.) The beam is an unbroken flow. It can't therefore be defined as some kind of one-off blitz! Feel the energy as it flows powerfully through you. It will often make itself felt as a warm tingling or, slightly less sharp but no less intensely, as a feeling of power and strength.

When you think you are capable of it, you can imagine this beam right from the start as appearing in a shimmering white color. Should you find this difficult, carry out the ritual for just a few weeks without imagining any color so you can then pick up the coloring procedure anew.

This is the union of macrocosm and microcosm, what Taoists call the "union of heaven and earth." In this way you harmonize your energies and establish harmony between your "above" and your "below." This part of the IAO Formula is also used for inspiration and opens up the crown chakra to your information universe.

The A Formula
Continuing to stand upright and with closed or half-closed eyes, stretch your arms out to the side and intone the vowel sound A (pronounced a as in "ah") in a long, drawn-out way:

"Aaaaaaaaaaaaahhhhhhh."

At the same time, imagine a continuous horizontal flow of energy that penetrates your body along the horizontal axis and shoots away to the right and left, and into the distance, which is where it also comes from. (This stream of light has no defined direction of flow. In fact it feels as if it is flowing simultaneously from left to right and from right to left.) Feel the energy as it powerfully flows through you. It will often make itself felt as a warm tingling or as a feeling of power and strength.

When you think you are capable of it, you can imagine this beam right from the start as appearing in a shimmering red color. Should you find this difficult, carry out the ritual just for a few weeks without imagining any color so you can then pick up the coloring procedure anew.

This is the union of the left and right sides, of giving and receiving, of action and endurance. (The Taoists speak of the "Union of Yin and Yang.") In this way you activate your powers and establish harmony between your "right" and your "left." This part of the IAO Protective Shield also serves to create mental and physical balance and opens up your hand chakras to your information universe.

The O Formula

Continuing to stand with closed or half-closed eyes, drop your arms back down to the side and intone the vowel sound O (pronounced *o* as in "oh") in a long, drawn-out way:

"Oooooooooooooohhhhh."

At the same time, imagine a continuous energy stream in the form of two circles orbiting around your body horizontally and vertically with a radius of about one and a half meters. (This stream of light has no defined direction of flow.

In fact, it feels as if it is flowing simultaneously to the right and to the left and from the top to the bottom and vice versa.) Feel the energy as it powerfully flows through you. It will often make itself felt as a warm tingling close to the skin or as a feeling of power and strength.

When you think you are capable of it, you can imagine this circular or spherical flow right from the start in a shimmering blue color. Should you find this difficult, carry out the ritual just for a few weeks without imagining any color so that you can then pick up the coloring procedure anew.

Now you can (with or without imagining the color)expand the O-circle or the double O-sphere outwards up to around six meters, depending upon how well you can maintain it. Note: These are only guidelines; if in doubt, you should follow your own intuition.

In this way you create an interior centering that resembles the drawing of a magic circle in its function. You concentrate your energies and position yourself at the center of your own cosmos. This part of the IAO Protective Shield Ritual also serves in the establishment of mental and physical balance, and of security and self-confidence. It reduces your magical vulnerability and makes you the ruler of your information universe.

The particular intonation you use must not be very loud. You should do your best to carry it out with as much power as possible, however. With some experience, you will work out the right volume, pitch, intonation, and duration of the intonation that suits you personally.

So the IAO Protective Shield works both for magical protection and also for centering and for power recharging. It can be practiced with success for healing purposes both by yourself and another person receiving healing. As well as that, it can be put into action at any time completely without risk and precisely when needed.

Figure 8 on the next page shows the sequence of the IAO Protective Shield Ritual.

Run through the IAO Protective Shield Ritual every time you bathe or shower while your body is still damp. Pay attention to your subtle perceptions, especially in your body: Where does the energy flow with each vowel? How do the three vowels differ in their effect? Also try to scan the energy ball with your eyes closed. What do you feel while doing it?

After awhile, you can perform the IAO Protective Shield Ritual as often as you want at every possible opportunity, for example after waking up in the morning or before you go to sleep, before a tricky conversation with your boss, with co-workers or relatives, before an exam or a court case, when setting off on a journey, and before facing challenges of any kind. It is suitable for use before and after the Ritual of the Pentagram, and indeed before and after every magical ceremony.

I: white
A: red
O: blue

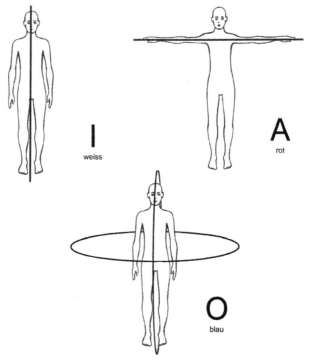

Figure 8: The IAO Protective Shield Ritual

THE THANATOS RITUAL

Thanatos is the ancient Greek name for the god of death. According to the belief system of the ancients, all life plays out between the two poles of *Eros* and *Thanatos*. Here, Eros embodies love, erotic attraction, and ultimately reproduction, hence life itself. *Thanatos* stands for death, disintegration, dissolution, and annihilation; in short, transience. This polarity has always been a core preoccupation for all cultures and civilizations. Ultimately, all religions have made death and the finite nature of the world their fundamental dilemmas.

The fear of death is a significant motivational force throughout human activity. From the prehistoric ancestor cults via the previously mentioned ancient Egyptian cult of the afterlife and the "art of dying" (*ars moriendi*) of the Christian Middle Ages, the metaphysical engagement with dying stretches as far as the promises we get today from technology for genetic immortality. Since the survival instinct is intrinsic to all people, the threat of death has always served as an effective instrument of deterrence for the exercise of authority and oppression.

On the other hand, many ingenious mechanisms have been developed to eliminate or displace the human fear of death. Thus it has to be overcome in favor of other priorities, for example, to awaken courage and defiance of death in military personnel, would-be assassins, and other groups, all of whom expose themselves to the greatest danger to life. Techniques for the suppression of the fear of death instinct include the administration of narcotics as well as indoctrination through the promise of an attractive reward waiting in the afterlife. One might include here the seventy-two virgins in paradise of jihadist attackers, the Roman *dulce et decorum est pro patria mori* ("it is sweet and honorable to die for one's fatherland"), the early Christian cult of martyrdom with its promise of eternal life, the sentiment expressed in the medals, titles, and monuments of state-run hero cults, and similar manipulative practices.

It is undeniable that the fear of death can paralyze us as well as make us highly vulnerable. One can see the opposite mechanism at work when it comes to the prevention of suicide attacks. Since these attackers don't seem to shy away from death at all but actively long for it, the standard deterrence measures appealing to their survival instinct are generally ineffective.

The fear of death has long been recognized and addressed in the most diverse cultures. For example, there is the symbolic "shamanic death" through which the shaman brings into being or consolidates his or her own active power. The biographies of many shamans also describe how the person only becomes a shaman once they have survived a lethal disease—with or without the healing intervention of another shaman. Here again we touch upon the concept that overcoming death makes a human being more powerful and even unassailable in a sense.

By "shamanic death," we are referring to a spiritual process, during the course of which the body and soul of the shaman runs through the whole death process on a symbolic-imaginative level, returning to everyday life afterward both purified and liberated. Here we see a significant mythological parallel with the sun gods of various cultures who likewise usually die and are then resurrected. The idea is pervasive, even today. As is well known, the whole theology of Christianity is founded upon the resurrection of Jesus Christ, without which (according to Christian dogma) there is no redemption of the world.

The Chöd ritual, very similar to these shamanic practices, is deeply rooted in Tibetan culture and strongly influenced by pre-Buddhist Bön beliefs as well as later Vajrayana or Tantric Buddhism. For this ritual, the practitioner makes their way to a secluded location in the wilderness over the course of an appropriate period of meditation, often many days, to symbolically offer up their body, limbs, and so on to the beasts and demons of the wild; thus they seek to be symbolically killed, torn apart, and annihilated.

The aim of these practices is to become aware of the finite nature of one's own existence through the experience of the most drastic soul drama possible, thus not to be limited any longer by life or by existence. Out of the experience, the adept doesn't just gain fearlessness—they also acquire impressive magical powers.

The comparatively young cult of *Santa Muerte* originally sprung up in Mexico from where it has now rapidly spread out into the neighboring Central American countries, and even into the United States. According to estimates, it can already count on ten million followers, a number that keeps growing daily. Outwardly this cult positions itself as Catholic, much to the chagrin of the Roman Catholic Church, which rejects the cult vehemently.

The reservation on the part of the Catholic Church is quite understandable, as this cult does actually make manifest to a large extent elements of the pre-Columbian Aztec (that is, pre-Christian and indigenous) religions of Central

America. The trappings of the faith of the church are only superficially maintained; for example, in the foundation of chapels, churches, and pilgrimage sites, the use of crucifixes, the organizing of processions, as well as the appropriation of numerous elements of Catholic Marian devotion.

If you consider the history of religion, the Santa Muerte cult, isolated precursors of which can be found in Mexico during the seventeenth century, is essentially a reworking (or from another point of view, a continuation) of the Aztec veneration of the ruler of the kingdom of the dead *Mictlantecuhtli* (also *Mictlantecuhtzi* or *Tzontemoc*) and his consort *Mictlancihuatl* (also *Mictecacihuatl* or *Mictlantecihuatl*). This does not prevent the majority of believers from considering themselves devout Catholics, however. Little difference does it make that they are vociferously reviled by the church as "Satanists" an even vehemently attacked via public mass exorcisms. What's more, they are frequently accused by the Catholic clergy of infiltration by violent drug cartels and even of human sacrifice.

It should be noted here that in the Romance languages, the word "death" is assigned the feminine gender, as it is in Mexican Spanish, so the name *Santa Muerte* can literally be translated as "Holy Lady Death." Incidentally, another name for Santa Muerte is *La Niña Blanca*, "the white girl", a way of describing her appearance as a pale skeleton. In this cult, death is revered like a Catholic saint; for example, by the burning of votive candles, the rendering of offerings like water and tequila (as a skeleton, so it's said, she constantly suffers from thirst), but also of cigarettes and money, through the creation and use of votive tablets, and so on. Unlike the official, canonical saints, Santa Muerte is not considered to be a historical person, but rather a personification of death itself.

Numerous miracles are attributed to Santa Muerte, and old folk magic practices also play out in her cult. For example, her followers might pray for the death of a sick relative to be deferred—or even to bring about the death of a rival or opponent. November 1 is celebrated throughout Mexico as a national holiday and festival of the dead—*Dia de los Muertos* (literally "day of the dead"), corresponding to All Saints' Day in the Catholic church calendar. Although not directly linked with the Santa Muerte cult, the holiday does hark back in the context of Mexican culture to pre-Columbian roots. The Aztecs dedicated the entire ninth month of their annual calendar to the kingdom of the dead and its ruling couple. This notion was thus taken in the course of the conquistadors led by the Catholic Church as an opportunity to replace this Pagan custom with particularly strong emphasis on the Christian All Saints' and All Souls' days, although their respective origins were quite different.

It is striking that death, in complete accordance with the Mesoamerican pre-Christian religious systems, is by no means seen to be merely negative. Rather it is considered to be an integral, affirmative part of life that is even celebrated as a form of expression of fertility. So on the *Dia de los Muertos,* you share decorated confections shaped as skeletons or skulls and themed flower arrangements, wear Grim Reaper costumes in processions, make your face up as a death mask, crack all kinds of jokes with relatives, friends, and neighbors about death or dead people, and so on. In this way, the figure of death becomes a protective goddess, who can be understood positively and with whom you can communicate and create a relationship, something profitable and enriching for humanity.

The following ritual is composed of elements from various cultures that all engage intensively with the theme of death. It serves to enhance a familiarity with death, having a constructive effect on our own lives. Like all rituals, this one should be conducted often to intensify the experience, make it into an integral part of your life, and thus reinforce your personal integrity. It remains up to you to determine the intervals between carrying it out. It should probably be enough to perform the ritual once a year—preferably, of course, on November 1.

Make sure that you will remain undisturbed for at least two to three hours. Prepare for the Thanatos meditation by setting something up as your death meditation object, something clearly visible in your meditation posture. This can be a miniature skeleton, a skull, a graphic, or imaginative representation of the Grim Reaper or—even better— a meditation object that has been created in connection with the Santa Muerte cult, for example, specifically prepared for this purpose. (At the end of this section you will find an illustration created with just this purpose in mind.)

First, take fifty calm and deep breaths while you gaze at the meditation object standing before you with your eyes wide open. While doing so, don't lose yourself in your thoughts and associations; let these go as they arise and then just disappear without attaching your attention to them. Instead pay attention to your breathing and nothing else. (In this way, the image of the meditation object also impresses itself better upon the subconscious part of your soul.)

Now start to change your breathing so that with each inhalation you symbolically soak up the image of the meditation object. Do this for as long as it takes until you feel completely inundated by it. This can happen very quickly, but it might also take awhile. In any case, make sure that this death representation effectively fills you up internally before you continue on to the next step.

Now shut your eyes and let the death, which you have thus taken on, get to work on you. Can you feel how flesh, skin, and bones are slowly detaching from each other? Watch the process like a neutral observer without giving in to emotions like fear or disquiet but at the same time without the arising of joy or exultation. The experience must not be dominated by any emotion. Do you notice how your inner organs are beginning to decompose? How your body is shrinking? How your limbs are starting to become detached? (Of course you are maintaining your peaceful, unhurried, and solid breathing. Your subconscious mind can live quite happily with this symbolic paradox!) Can you feel now how your flesh is starting to decay? How the bodily fluids are leaving the organism? How the internal organs and blood are liquefying into formless clumps? Perhaps the smell of decay is starting to pervade? (Again it's important not to indulge any emotions, therefore no disgust or terror.) Can you feel how all the bonds to life are unraveling—material, idealistic, and human/social?

Keep carrying on with this until the process is thoroughly complete. Furthermore, the neutral observer inside you is engaged with registering the effective power of the active death principle in a sober manner.

Only when you are sure you feel that the process has reached its conclusion, breathe quickly three times through your nose and open your eyes again abruptly. Now you can get back up, put away the meditation object, and move on to something else.

Performing a symbolic act of revitalization and resurrection is *not* part of the Thanatos ritual. It is not required because you rose again straight away and seamlessly continued with your daily life after the complete meditation. It may be that you enjoy this practice and you might want to carry it out as often as possible, at least initially. On principle there's no reason you can't, as long as you don't carry it to excess. Because at this stage it's not a matter of getting attached to a different perspective on death and impermanence. In that case, the precise opposite of what the ritual was actually aiming for would have been achieved. There are no rigid dogmatic directions for this either, as it can be expressed quite differently, depending on the individual. Perhaps in this case you could take it as a rule of thumb that you should stick to performing the ritual just once a week. This piece of advice is necessary because the Thanatos Ritual—from previous experience—can have a tremendously alluring effect on some people; overindulgence in it is strongly discouraged.

Figure 9: Thanatos

Figure 9 shows an image made by the Berlin artist and Voodoo magician Hagen von Tulien. He has created—especially for the Thanatos Ritual outlined earlier—a limited edition meditation object (not shown here) the use of which we highly recommend to you without reservation. You can find a brief biography and contact details for the artist in the list of sources at the end of the book.

Protocols
PROTOCOL CHAPTER 7–1

00.00–00.50 (50') *Phase 1*: Lying down

00.50–02.00 (70') *Phase 2*: Marking your boundaries L

02.00–02.15 (15') *Phase 3*: Note taking while walking around

02.15–03.20 (65') *Phase 4*: Lying down

03.20–03.40 (20') *Phase 5*: Orienting yourself by your avoidance direction

03.40–04.20 (40') *Phase 6*: Greater mudra

04.20–05.00 (40') *Phase 7*: Technical sleep

05.00–05.55 (55') *Phase 8*: Lesser mudra 3

05.55–06.10 (15') *Phase 9*: Note taking while walking around

06.10–06.34 (24') *Phase 10*: Standing

06.34–07.00 (26') *Phase 11*: Lesser mudra 2

07.00–07.50 (50') *Phase 12*: Systematic pressure point change

07.50–08.05 (15') *Phase 13*: Lying down

08.05–09.05 (60') *Phase 14*: Report

Explanations
Lying down. On your back (if necessary slightly skewed to the right), outwardly motionless, alert.

Marking your boundaries L. A precise assessment takes place in the lying down position, of where the "alien" and "home" begin and continue on. While doing it you begin at first with the body. The relevant areas are then also extended, as the case may be. In the note taking and reporting phases, the results are then documented in a schematic and graphic sketch.

Note taking while walking around. For this protocol, you abandon your original position and work while standing or walking. You can walk up and down the room, or visit the toilet, etc. This helps with the production of additional self-alignment possibilities once you have returned to your lying down position.

In addition to that, you can use the time to make written notes, draw sketches etc., which you can draw upon for hints at the end of the overall summing up in your reporting session.

Orienting yourself by your avoidance direction. In the lying down position, determine your current overall body direction (e.g., the situation as determined by gravity) and immediately just on the impulse level, meaning without making any outward movement, turn in the other direction. If this is successful, then take a bearing once again upon the currently opposing direction on the impulse level, and so on.

Greater mudra. In a sitting position, let your upper arms rest gently against your torso. Touch the fingertips of both hands (all ten fingers, i.e., including the thumbs) gently against each other, thus forming pairs. First, reduce the pressure between the fingers of one pair, and then let it go completely while still maintaining the contact between them. Eventually, carry out the same procedure with four fingertips, two further pairs, until at the end all the fingertips are still resting against each other but without expending any pressure. Should the fingertips become separated from each other, you must start the greater mudra all over again.

Note: You should make sure that this does *not* become a matter of imagining (whether it's figurative or abstract/mental) but instead that it's a genuine bodily and sensation-based operation.

Technical sleep. The aim here is to cross over directly into the sleep state without a transitional stage (gradual darkening, etc.). It is to be expected that this (initially) won't be successful, but if so, continue to make an unbroken effort to get closer to it.

Lesser mudra 1. In a sitting position, rest your upper arms against the sides of your body, and touch the tips of one pair of fingers (e.g., your index fingers) gently against each other. Reduce the pressure between the fingers, then let it go completely while *still* maintaining the contact between them. Should the fingertips become separated from each other, you must start the lesser mudra all over again.

Note: You should make sure that this does *not* become a matter of imagining (whether it's figurative or abstract/mental) but instead that it's a genuine bodily and sensation-based operation.

Lesser mudra number… See above. The numbers are there to indicate how many pairs of fingers to work with. With the number 2, that means two pairs (the index and ring fingers for example), with the number 3, three, and with the number 4, four pairs of fingers. No thumbs are used!

Standing. Stand up straight with your feet a shoulder width apart and your back straight but not strained. Don't make any effort to outwardly maintain your position without making any movement.

Systematic pressure point change
While lying down, define five points on the body:

> *Right heel*
> *Left heel*
> *Right shoulder*
> *Left shoulder*
> *The middle of the back of your head*

Over the course of the protocol, place your attention first upon pressure point 1 (right heel). This body point is to be determined precisely. Once this has happened (or your attention loosens or you find it starts wandering), change it over to pressure point 2 (left heel). Do the same thing here, until the pressure point has either been precisely determined and narrowed down or your attention lets go or wanders. Then direct your attention towards pressure point 3 (right shoulder) and continue proceeding accordingly. Pressure point 4 (left shoulder) follows, and then pressure point 5 (the middle of the back of your head). Once you have done all you can at pressure point 5, direct your attention back towards pressure point 1, and the cycle begins anew.

Note: It is important to make sure that when determining the pressure points you don't treat them imaginatively (be it as an image or abstractly in your mind), but as tangible objects, which you can define with your senses!

PROTOCOL CHAPTER 7–2

00.00–02.00 (120') *Phase 1*: Walking a short space using impulsing

02.00–02.30 (30') *Phase 2*: Lying down

02.30–02.45 (15') *Phase 3*: Flat walking 100%

02.45–03.15 (30') *Phase 4*: Flat walking 50%

03.15–03.20 (5') *Phase 5*: Flat walking 33%

03.20–03.35 (15') *Phase 6*: Note taking while walking around

03.35–04.20 (45') *Phase 7*: Lying down

04.20–05.35 (75') *Phase 8*: Impulse circulation

05.35–06.35 (60') *Phase 9*: Report

Walking a short space using impulsing. This consists of two subphases (1.1 and 1.2) as follows.

Sub-phase 1.1—Preparation (30'): Determine a spot that's three or four paces away from where you are and then mark it. Try walking it out once and then remove the mark.

Sub-phase 1.2—Main Part (90'): Starting from a lying down position, leave the place you are in without any external movement (see Impulse Circulation) and take the steps you decided upon in sub-phase 1.1. Then return again to your starting position and lie down, and then stand up again immediately, walk that stretch, etc.

Note: As the walking a short space using an impulsing protocol is accomplished *without any external movement,* it takes place just on the levels of motoric impulse. You must ensure that this is *not* just an act of imagining (be it as an image or abstractly in your mind), but a genuine physical (although purely "internal") impulsing!

Lying down. On your back (if necessary slightly skewed to the right), outwardly motionless, alert.

Flat walking 100 percent. Cover a determined distance at a normal walking pace. This is to be carried out initially with a normal downward pressure of the soles of the feet, in order to determine the (subjective) reference value of 100% pressure expenditure.

Flat walking 50 percent. Like 1, but with half the downward pressure (50 percent) in comparison with the previously established reference value.

Flat walking 33 percent. Like 1, but with one-third the downward pressure (33 percent) in comparison with the previously established reference value.

You can proceed accordingly with further percentage figures. (So, "10 percent" means 10 percent pressure expenditure, always in comparison to the previously established reference value, as you continue.)

Tip: Take care to work *with* gravity instead of against it.

Note taking while walking around. For this protocol, you abandon your original position and work while standing or walking. You can walk up and down the room or visit the toilet, etc. This helps with the production of additional self-alignment possibilities once you have returned to your lying down position.

In addition to that, you can use the time to make written notes, draw sketches, etc., which you can draw upon for hints at the end of the overall summary in your reporting session.

Impulse circulation. Standing up *without any outward body movement* with an immediate return to a lying down position before any bodily reaction occurs.

Note: Impulse circulation is accomplished *without any external movement*; it takes place just on the levels of motoric impulse. You must ensure that this is *not* a matter of an act of imagining (be it as an image or abstractly in your mind), but a genuine physical (although purely "internal") impulsing!

PROTOCOL CHAPTER 7–3

00.00–01.40 (100') *Phase 1*: Lying down

01.40–02.10 (30') *Phase 2*: Impulsing in circular phases 7/7

02.10–02.20 (10') *Phase 3*: Note taking while walking around

02.20–03.00 (40') *Phase 4*: Steering fingers

03.00–03.15 (15') *Phase 5*: Note taking while walking around

03.15–03.40 (25') *Phase 6*: Impulsing in circular phases 6/6

03.40–04.10 (30') *Phase 7*: Lying down

04.10–04.30 (20') *Phase 8*: Greater mudra

04.30–05.15 (45') *Phase 9*: Lying down

05.15–06.15 (60') *Phase 10*: Collision empowerment

06.15–06.45 (30') *Phase 11*: Lying down

06.45–07.30 (45') *Phase 12*: Orienting yourself by your avoidance direction

07.30–08.15 (45') *Phase 13*: Lying down

08.15–09.15 (60') *Phase 14*: Report

Explanations

Lying down. On your back (if necessary slightly skewed to the right), outwardly motionless, alert.

Impulsing in circular phases. An alternation between lying down and/or sleeping, and activities done while standing up, divided into phases. The latter can be performed using any activities you like, and the digits following indicate the value in minutes of the particular phases (5/5 = five minutes sleep/ five minutes standing up, etc.).

Note taking while walking around. For this protocol, you abandon your original position and work while standing or walking. You can walk up and down the room, or visit the toilet, etc. This helps with the production of additional self-alignment possibilities once you have returned to your lying down position.

In addition to that, you can use the time to make written notes, draw sketches, etc., which you can draw upon for hints at the end of the overall summing up in your reporting session.

Steering fingers. Write by hand on an 8½ by 11-inch piece of paper, for up to 30 minutes, eyes closed, on a theme of your own choosing.

Greater mudra. In a sitting position, let your upper arms rest gently against your torso. Touch the fingertips of both hands (so all ten fingers, i.e., including the thumbs) gently against each other, thus forming pairs. Then first of all reduce the pressure between the fingers of one pair, and next let it go completely, while still maintaining the contact between them. Eventually, carry out the same procedure with four fingertips, thus two further pairs, until at the end all the fingertips are still resting against each other, but without expending any pressure. Should the fingertips become separated from each other, you must start the greater mudra all over again.

Note: You should make sure that this does *not* become a matter of imagining (whether it's figurative or abstract/mental) but instead that it's a genuine bodily and sensation-based operation.

Collision empowerment. To be carried out in three sub-phases:

Sub-phase 1.1—Deciding on an object: Pick an immobile object and take up a standing position a few steps away from it.

Sub-phase 1.2—Align yourself towards a collision point, 100% distance away: Keeping your stance outwardly motionless, align yourself towards a collision with the object. You should ensure that this does *not* become a matter of imagination (whether it's figurative or abstract/mental), but instead that it's a genuine, inner-body, motoric process! Once the collision arc has been completely dealt with on a subjective basis, continue on to the next sub-phase.

Sub-phase 1.3—Align yourself towards a collision point, now 50% distance away: Reduce by half your distance away from the object. Then carry out the same procedure as described under 1.2.

Once you have exhausted the last sub-phase, perform the procedure as above with a different object.

Orienting yourself by your avoidance direction. In the lying down position, determine your current overall body direction (e.g., the situation as determined by gravity) and immediately just on the impulse level, meaning without making any outward movement, turn in the other direction. If this is successful, then take a bearing once again upon the currently opposing direction on the impulse level, and so on.

Protocol Chapter 7–4

00.00–00.45 (45') *Phase 1*: Lying down

00.45–01.00 (15') *Phase 2*: Applying pressure 100%

01.00–01.20 (20') *Phase 3*: Applying pressure 50%

01.20–01.40 (20') *Phase 4*: Applying pressure 33%

01.40–02.00 (20') *Phase 5*: Applying pressure 10%

02.00–02.15 (15') *Phase 6*: Note taking while walking around

02.15–03.30 (75') *Phase 7*: Lying down

03.30–03.35 (5') *Phase 8*: Picking up/putting down 100%

03.35–03.42 (7') *Phase 9*: Picking up/putting down 50%

03.42–03.49 (7') *Phase 10*: Picking up/putting down 33%

03.49–03.56 (7') *Phase 11*: Picking up/putting down 10%

03.56–04.20 (24') *Phase 12*: Note taking while walking around

04.20–04.50 (30') *Phase 13*: Shallow breathing

04.50–05.50 (60') *Phase 14*: Lying down

05.50–06.50 (60') *Phase 15*: Report

Explanations

Lying Down. On your back (if necessary slightly skewed to the right), outwardly motionless, alert.

1. *Applying pressure 100 percent.* In an upright position, legs a shoulder width apart, clasping an object in both hands and holding it clear in front of your body, without being supported by anything. This is first of all carried out with normal pressure, to maintain a (subjective) reference value of 100 percent expenditure of pressure.

2. *Applying pressure 50 percent.* Just like point one, but with half the amount of pressure expenditure (50 percent) in relation to the previously established reference value.

3. *Applying pressure 33 percent.* Just like point one, but with one-third the amount of pressure expenditure (33 percent) in relation to the previously established reference value.

4. *Applying pressure 10 percent.* Just like point one, but with one-tenth the amount of pressure expenditure (10 percent) in relation to the previously established reference value.

It is recommended you should use as the object something like an unbreakable plastic bottle filled with fresh water that has been tightly closed beforehand. This will help in the event of the object slipping from your grip, thereby avoiding accidents with broken glass shards, injuries, as well as other damage.

It will turn out that over time the bottle will threaten to slip out of your hands. In fact, the use of a "deep grip" (that is, by using an ever stronger pressure) will also not permanently stop this process. ("In the depths, the grip gets lost.") For that reason, it's a matter of abandoning pressure exertion if possible when you are holding on and, instead, of developing an alternative form of grip.

Tip: Do your best to work *with* gravity, rather than against it.

Note taking while walking around. For this protocol, you abandon your original position and work while standing or walking. You can walk up and down the room, visit the toilet, etc. This helps with the production of additional self-alignment possibilities once you have returned to your lying down position.

In addition to that, you can use the time to make written notes, draw sketches, etc., which you can draw upon for hints at the end of the overall summary in your reporting session.

1. *Picking up/putting down 100 percent.* Move an object around in various ways; rearrange it, twist it around, put it away, etc. Carry this out initially at normal speed, to maintain a (subjective) reference value of full speed.

2. *Picking up/putting down 50 percent.* Just like point one, but with half the speed (50 percent) in relation to the previously established reference value.

3. *Picking up/putting down 33 percent.* Just like point one, but with one-third the speed (33 percent) in relation to the previously established reference value.

You can proceed accordingly with further percentage figures. (So, "10 percent" means 10 percent of the speed, always in comparison to the previously established reference value, and so on.)

Shallow breathing. Make your breathing as shallow as possible in this lying down position, without becoming tense.

8

PROTECTIVE AND HELPFUL BEINGS

"Angels" and "Demons,"
Your Most Powerful Allies

Since time immemorial, humanity has expended a large amount of attention on engaging with subtle beings normally invisible to the naked eye. Whether they are called ghosts, devils, daimons (good) or demons (bad), angels or power animals, goblins, sylphs, naiads or elementals, and whatever else you might want to call them—we are always dealing with entities, which are commonly deemed supernatural, ethereal, or hidden.

The existence and qualities, abilities, and intentions of these creatures have marked the religions and cults of past times. Still today many Jews, Christians, and Muslims, as well as Hindus and the followers of animistic cults (in Africa, Asia,

Papua New Guinea, Latin America, the Caribbean) have a basic starting position which says that spirits play a major role in the world's overall framework. Depending on their character and integration into higher contexts (the divine plan for the world, a dualistic conflict-drama between good and evil, redemption schemata), they are considered to be more or less powerful, influential, helpful, and even harmful as well. For example, illnesses often were and still are attributed to some kind of harmful or evil entity, and sometimes it is believed that ignorant spirits make themselves at home in the body of a sick person or in some way blunder their way into the body—that is, if the spirit wasn't loosed upon them by an adversary with the help of destructive spells. Accordingly, the healing treatment also often takes on the character of an exorcism, with the unwanted creatures needing to be expelled from the body and soul of the affected person. In the realm of Christian culture this is vouched for by the account in the New Testament (Mark, chapter 5), which tells of how the Nazarene healed one such person possessed by a plague of spirits by banishing them into a herd of swine. And it's not just the Catholic Church that still carries out numerous exorcisms upon its believers—even among evangelical Christians are numerous groups for which exorcism constitutes a regular religious practice.

Rationalism, materialism, and especially atheism of course, take no interest in these matters. On the other hand, the depth psychology of, say, C. G. Jung assumes a more ambivalent position regarding it. Jungian psychology does not explicitly deny the experience of the world of spirits, and many people today bring back reports from there. At the same time, it usually traces these kinds of experiences back to interior spiritual processes without committing itself to the possibility that these could also be treated as objective phenomena unequivocally. Even parapsychology, which has somewhat fallen into oblivion in recent years, to adopt a neutral, empirical, perspective when it comes to researching poltergeist phenomena: it is a perspective that chooses not to commit to a clear statement on the subject.

At this point, it should be noted that there are a multiplicity of approaches to understanding and interpreting such beings. If you should prefer to treat the subject purely psychologically, you are still at liberty to do so in conjunction with some kind of firm belief, for example, in guardian angels, astral larvae, or the devil. If you happen to subscribe to either view, you will find yourself in the best of company.

We have been able to observe that for millennia humanity has considered the ghost and spirit model for explaining the world to be manifestly helpful. The presence of guardian spirits or of a divine authority (perhaps even several) who watch over the welfare—yes, even the capability for survival—of individuals is felt to be very calming and stress reducing. After all, belief in the existence of harmful and threatening entities offers us the opportunity to personify challenges, difficulties, and dangers, making them easier to address.

For this reason, strategies can be developed for a productive interaction with them because protective beings, just like threatening ones, are clearly defined and often accurately named and described precisely when it comes to their qualities. From a pragmatic point of view, it makes absolutely no difference whether such beings are "real" or not. It is enough that they count as genuine for the person concerned in as much as belief facilitates an outlook that allows the person to engage with the spirit constructively.

Admittedly this is easier said than done. Because a belief in, say, evil spirits and demons can often be articulated through vague fears and nightmares to which the person concerned sees themselves to be helplessly exposed. They feel subjectively powerless and often become an easy victim for charlatans and established priestly castes, which in reality are only pursuing their own profits while pretending to afford them assistance. Here too we must of course warn against undifferentiated generalizations. It can hardly be denied that the pastoral counsel of a priest, shaman, or guru is of great value to many people, even if in such a case the skeptic or atheist might only recognize the "opiate of the people" at work. We really won't get very far though with these kinds of value judgments.

Chaos magic is preoccupied with this problem in a postmodern, fractured way. Although it does not postulate the existence of spirits and other supernatural beings, it also doesn't rule out the ability of the magician to create a kind of "chaos servitor" by means of the appropriate practices to use it for his or her own purposes. The question of the "real (objective) existence" of these beings thus moves into the background, as it's generally considered not to be essential. Conceptually neither ghosts (the spiritual model in magic) nor powers (the energy model) play a role here, just as interior soul processes (the psychological model) don't either. Instead of this, one assumes a magical handling of information (the information model). This is based upon the mindset of quantum mechanics, without however actually having anything to do with quantum physics in an academic sense.

In the ancient Egyptian Book of the Dead (*pert em heru,* "The Book of Coming Forth by Day"), you can find the statement: "A deity dwells in every part of your body." So now the human being is itself a place of habitation for supernatural beings. Therefore, it is not the case that they would invariably enter the body only from the outside.

The German chemist and secondary school teacher Ludwig Staudenmeier practiced forms of possession magic shortly before the first World War that initially resulted in 1910 in an extensive scientific paper, and later in his magnum opus, *Magic as Experimental Science,* republished on many occasions and expanded once more in 1922. His many years of extensive self-experimentation, a thing he himself described as the production of an "artificial schizophrenia," can be interpreted psychoanalytically as an exercise in targeted splitting of the personality. This shows clear parallels with Babylonian demonology. With Staudenmaier we also find, as is likewise indicated in the Egyptian Book of the Dead, a physical localization of beings visible to him, which he is convinced can also manifest externally/materially.

However, it should not go unmentioned that Staudenmaier was repeatedly admitted for inpatient psychiatric care based on diagnosed schizophrenia, which did eventually make him incapable of working. The question in this case of what was cause and what effect, meaning whether it was latent at first and then these experiences caused an acute outbreak of schizophrenia, or whether it occurred in exactly the opposite fashion: that he induced this split personality in the first place through his continued experimentation, will in all likelihood never be properly clarified.

To deviate from our previous way of proceeding, in this chapter we will first of all deal with the spiritual, then with the mental and right at the end with the physical aspect of the subject. The reason for this is that we are by definition dealing with a primarily spiritual phenomenon that requires the corresponding experiences for the appropriate mental and physical ones to be integrated as a consequence.

Soul: The Handling of Protective Spirits

You can also interpret the "protective entities" we will go on to discuss in the following pages in a purely symbolic/psychological way. In which case they might be regarded as personified aspects of your soul, which can then be addressed, but which need to have a "real" materially manifest existence on the "outside." The advantages and the limitations of this approach will be considered in the "Mind" section.

We are mentioning this approach to the relevant meanings right at the start, because frankly it needs explaining to most contemporary readers. Many would harbor major discomfort if it were expected for them to believe in the existence of ghosts and demons. It would only lead to unnecessary stress, as what's important is definitely not certain aspects of what you believe but the dimension of how you experience the related practices.

On the other hand, you need not adapt yourself agonizingly to some kind of depth psychology model if it doesn't particularly sit well with you simply because the genuine objective existence of such entities is for you an undisputed fact. If that's the case for you, only concern yourself with the technical execution of the practices presented here all the same.

Finally, it is also conceivable that you might not settle on one or the other point of view. That is also not absolutely necessary as long as you bring with you one thing, namely *open-minded curiosity*. If you take note of your unbiased experiences right from the start, you will draw your own conclusions from them regardless, and then they are unlikely to retain any longer the character of untested speculations.

Should you have made contact with some kind of protective being already, you can skip the following protective spirit meditation. In this case it won't be necessary unless you have high hopes of getting additional insights from it.

THE PROTECTIVE SPIRIT MEDITATION

Make sure that you will be undisturbed for one to two hours. Assume a comfortable sitting position (if you have relevant yoga experience, try the half-lotus or ruler position) and take around one hundred deep and calm breaths. Simply drop any thoughts that arise without getting mixed up with them, but also without actively trying to drive them out. Just concentrate on your breathing.

Once you have performed the designated number of breaths, visualize a silvery-bright beam of light, which, slowly coming down from above, enters through the top of your head and moves at a leisurely pace downwards through the middle of your body, to exit it finally at your coccyx and then sink into the ground. Maintain this beam for as long as you are performing the meditation.

Continue to breathe calmly and deeply, but now apply all your attention to the beam of light. Once this image has stabilized, turn your attention to the mid-point between your eyes and inside the head. (At this point your eyes are closed.) Now add another component to the meditation by simultaneously letting a sense of being *protected* arise that surrounds you like a sphere (meanwhile the light beam is still being maintained, the point between the eyes is fixed from this point on). Are you still noticing how the beam of light flows through from above to below, or how the light at the point between your eyes is becoming concentrated? What about how protection now sheaths the outside of your body so that ultimately it will penetrate it entirely?

Maintain this state for between twenty and fifty breaths. In the meantime, you shouldn't be actively counting your breaths in case you become distracted. A rough sense of the required length of time is completely sufficient.

It's possible that you might suddenly see a form, shape, face, or something else tangibly before your inner eye that you recognize clearly and distinctly. Or you might also hear an interior voice, sound, melody, or even a clearly spoken statement. Perhaps the being you have perceived will share its name or otherwise start a dialogue with you. Even sensations of smell can't be ruled out either on their own or alongside other perceptions.

Most people have completely varied experiences: For as long as the sense of protection has been meaningfully established, it will often be the case that no additional images, sounds, smells, or taste phenomena will occur. So this is not the exception but rather the norm. In this respect, you do not need to feel disappointed or doubt your abilities in case this could restrict your experience.

Once you have carried out the meditation as described, open your eyes and get back up. Now occupy yourself with something else for at least five minutes without any further reflection on the meditation. You could go to the bathroom, empty the trash, or gather up the laundry. The more banal and mundane the activity, the better. The aim here is not active forgetting as with the sigil magic, but rather the most seamless dovetailing possible with your normal daily activities.

Mind: The Psychological Advantages of a Mental Model—and How You Can Use it Successfully and Effortlessly in Everyday Situations

We have already alluded to this idea several times: By allowing interior spiritual issues and processes to be personified, they become addressable and therefore manageable. The scapegoat of the Israelite tribes in the Old Testament is a well-known example. Once a year, the sins of the whole nation were transferred onto a goat that was then chased out into the wilderness. Thus the people were symbolically "cleansed" and no longer needed to feel burdened by any feelings of guilt and remorse. The situation is similar with the personification of fears and traumas, as we apply the process today in certain psychotherapeutic movements in order to help clients or patients with confronting them and depriving them of their active power.

From a psychological perspective, these are purely symbolic actions that have nothing to do with the question of whether or not there *really* are such personified demons or "evil spirits." The only thing that's significant is that the human psyche gets a handle on it by doing this so that it can free itself from compulsions, pressure, pain, and suffering. The key element here is the *addressability*.

So when, for example, atheists and rationalists make a huge fuss about underlining the absurdity of spiritual belief, and impute gullibility, ignorance, or stupidity upon its adherents, they are merely ignorant of the actual issue at hand. Addressability means, for example, that spiritual healing powers can organize around one purpose that commands clear contours and thus makes it possible to impose a clear direction upon the healing process. That may or may not be an only slightly evolved or even a downright primitive approach. From a pragmatic point of view, it is nevertheless considerably more meaningful and promising than when a disaster that could easily be averted instead remains vague and indeterminate, with the powers of healing potential going astray due to sheer lack of focus and direction.

From a magical information point of view, the effort to facilitate the effectiveness of every assumed outfit and every mask that might help ensure the desired success should therefore always remain in the foreground. Also from this viewpoint the question of the objective "reality" of such spiritual phenomena does not even arise. "Reality" is always that which exerts an effect upon us in a "real" i.e., tangible sense regardless of what costume it turns up wearing or through what specific set of glasses it wants to be viewed.

Body: A Bodily Anchor for the Manufacture and Strengthening of the Bond with Protective Entities ("Angels" and "Demons")

Once you have finished the protective spirit meditation, take a few minutes when you are outwardly undisturbed to see to the creation of a physical anchor. To do this you certainly shouldn't pick up the meditation again, but rather summon up once more the feeling of protection you have already induced. This can be done discreetly while sitting down, lying in bed, or even during a quiet minute at breakfast. If the feeling of protection in all its aspects starts to fall back into place, something that at first is technically nothing more than an act of remembrance, then either formulate a mudra as you have already done earlier in the course of this procedure, or anchor this experience with another physical gesture that should be as unobtrusive as possible. For example, you could contract an underarm muscle while you simultaneously maintain that protected feeling and then release it again, briefly tense up the muscles at the back of your neck or quickly but unnoticeably clamp your teeth together. The nature of the anchoring is not important, as long as you can recall it once again without great effort. If you have had to deal with a perceptively manifest being during your protective spirit meditation, you should of course incorporate it into this anchoring, while you maintain at the same time this feeling of protection. That's all there is to it!

When you reactivate your mudra or your physical anchor the next day or on any of the days that follow, the feeling of protection, which you previously evoked in your protective spirit meditation, should arise again, too. Maybe this won't work the first or second time. If so, start the whole thing over again as required for you to feel satisfied with the outcome.

You have now effectively extended your protective arsenal. Whenever you find yourself under threat, if anxiety (undirected) or fear (directed) threaten to gain the upper hand or you are expecting a challenge or an attack from adversaries, activate this anchor. It should significantly strengthen your resistance and assertiveness capabilities.

Self-Initiation

What we have lent the somewhat presumptuous designator "Self-Initiation" is actually nothing more than the integration and rounding-off of the practices and procedures presented in this book. The goal here then is not to run through a process defined by any given hierarchical framework of stages or grades as you would perhaps in a magical order or mystery school. Way more than that, it's a process of closing down and a simultaneous opening. First of all, your "old" previous life is closed down—it was a life in which the sayings, the recommendations and the instructions we have since covered here had yet to play any role. That's nothing dramatic in itself; it's not a rebirth or enlightenment as these moments can often be described. It was really only the sober recognition of a learning process, something that should lead you further along your particular life path.

It's an "opening," in the sense that a rich field for the investigation of new, hitherto largely or completely unknown approaches to life and ways of increasing your efficiency have now opened up to you, just waiting for you to explore them. Thus the world can become a single field of experimentation, in which you will increasingly broaden your capabilities, consolidate your self-protection and the protection of others close to you, and successfully realize your concerns and interests.

Make sure you will be undisturbed for between one and two hours. Assume a comfortable sitting position (perhaps in the half-lotus or ruler positions, if you have the appropriate yoga experience) and take around fifty quiet and deep breaths.

Now call to mind your basic training. How exactly did you carry it out? What experiences did you have while doing it? What difficulties did you encounter? How did you handle them? Which aspects did you actually deal with thoroughly, and which still need to be thoroughly dealt with?

Now go through the next part of the work you underwent here. Examine it using the same set of questions. Then the next. Then the next one after that and so on.

Finally consider how you would like to go on from here. What areas interest you the most? Where do you still have gaps in your knowledge that you would like to fill? How exactly will you do that? What in the future would you rather not deal with? Why not? What is attracting your attention most strongly? Why is that? In the future, what would you like to start working on in a concrete way with regard to what you have learned? If you have worked with one or more training partners whether only occasionally or on a regular basis, do you think you will continue with this? Similarly, if you have been working without a training partner, will you continue to work alone or try instead with one or more training partners?

Be gentle with yourself. You don't need to make any value judgments; cultivating self-reproach and remorse and an avoidance of any improvement is never required of you. If you are honest with yourself, you will probably realize that you have only actually mastered a fraction of the curriculum presented here. Take note of this, register it, but don't dwell on it. Draw your conclusions from it. Maybe you want to stop completely. Then do so. Do you want to know and learn even more? Then just make every effort to do so.

In doing this, you have not initiated yourself into any kind of new system of spiritual or magical development that has been laid down by someone else. You have not been initiated *into* something so much as *toward* something different—your own self-empowerment.

In conclusion, there only remains for us to say that we wish you every conceivable success on your journey!

Protocols
Protocol Chapter 8–1
00.00–02.00 (120') *Phase 1*: Forest walk 2 (Ghost Step)
02.00–03.00 (60') *Phase 2*: Report

Explanations
Forest Walk 2 (Ghost Step). A previously determined, tried, and tested woodland path is followed at nighttime, divided into various sub-phases as follows.

Sub-phase 2.1—Weight displacement equalization (30'): While making a stride, initially put your center of gravity completely over the leading foot. Then, after a short pause, relocate it—with as little impetus as possible—to a position above the following foot. After a short pause while you transfer the pressure, move the following foot forward again, and so on.

Sub-phase 2.2—Striding (70'): Walk the next section of the track at a calm pace. While doing so, keep your attention as exclusively as possible upon your own sequence of movement. External distractions should be registered as seamlessly and as free from reflection as possible, without having a negative effect on you keeping your attention upon your walking.

Sub-phase 2.3—Weight displacement equalization (20'): Like 2.1.

PROTOCOL CHAPTER 8–2

00.00–01.50 (110') *Phase 1:* Lying down

01.50–02.55 (65') *Phase 2:* Impulse circulation

02.55–03.10 (15') *Phase 3:* Note taking while walking around

03.10–04.00 (50') *Phase 4:* Lying down

04.00–04.40 (40') *Phase 5:* Sitting

04.40–04.55 (15') *Phase 6:* Note taking while walking around

04.55–05.40 (45') *Phase 7:* Lying down

05.40–06.00 (20') *Phase 8:* Standing

06.00–06.15 (15') *Phase 9:* Note taking while walking around

06.15–07.10 (55') *Phase 10:* Lying down

07.10–08.10 (60') *Phase 11:* Report

Explanations

Lying down. On your back (if necessary slightly skewed to the right), outwardly motionless, alert.

Impulse circulation. Standing up *without any outward body movement,* with an immediate return to a lying down position before any bodily reaction occurs.

Note: As impulse circulation is accomplished *without any external movement* it takes place just on the levels of motoric impulse. You must ensure that this is *not* a matter of an act of imagining (be it as an image or abstractly in your mind), but a genuine physical (although purely "internal") impulsing!

Note taking while walking around. For this protocol, you abandon your original position and work while standing or walking. You can walk up and down the room, or visit the toilet, etc. This helps with the production of additional self-alignment possibilities once you have returned to your lying down position.

In addition to that, you can use the time to write notes, draw sketches, etc., which you can draw upon for hints at the end of the overall summary in your reporting session.

Sitting. In a seated position, rest your feet flat on the floor, your legs not touching each other, and your back in a comfortable upright posture without leaning on the back of the chair. Your effort is focused on keeping your position outwardly completely motionless.

Standing. Stand up straight with your feet a shoulder width apart and your back straight but not strained. Don't make any effort to outwardly maintain your position without making any movement.

PROTOCOL CHAPTER 8–3

00.00–02.20 (140') *Phase 1*: Lying down

02.20–02.30 (10') *Phase 2*: Pressure empowerment 100%

02.30–02.45 (15') *Phase 3*: Pressure empowerment 50%

02.45–03.05 (20') *Phase 4*: Pressure empowerment 25%

03.05–03.15 (10') *Phase 5*: Pressure empowerment 10%

03.15–03.35 (20') *Phase 6*: Note taking while walking around

03.35–04.15 (40') *Phase 7*: Lying down

04.15–04.45 (30') *Phase 8*: Standing

04.45–05.45 (60') *Phase 9*: Marking your boundaries L.

05.45–06.05 (20') *Phase 10*: Note taking while walking around

06.05–06.45 (40') *Phase 11*: Lying down

06.45–07.45 (60') *Phase 12*: Report

Lying down. On your back (if necessary slightly skewed to the right), outwardly motionless, alert.

1. *Pressure empowerment 100 percent.* In an upright position, legs a shoulder width apart, clasping an object in both hands and holding it clear in front of your body, without being supported by anything. This is first of all carried out with normal pressure, to maintain a (subjective) reference value of 100 percent expenditure of pressure.

2. *Pressure empowerment 50 percent.* Just like point one, but with half the amount of pressure expenditure (50 percent) in relation to the previously established reference value.

3. *Pressure empowerment 33 percent.* Just like point one, but with one-third the amount of pressure expenditure (33 percent) in relation to the previously established reference value.

4. *Pressure empowerment 10 percent.* Just like point one, but with one-tenth the amount of pressure expenditure (10 percent) in relation to the previously established reference value.

It is recommended that you should use something like an unbreakable plastic bottle filled with fresh water, that's been tightly closed beforehand as the object. This way, if the object slips, you won't have broken glass shards, resultant injuries, or other damage.

It will turn out that over time the bottle will threaten to slip out of your hands. In fact, using a "deep grip" (that is, by using an ever stronger pressure) will also not permanently stop this process. ("In the depths, the grip gets lost.") For that reason, it's a matter of abandoning pressure exertion if possible when you are holding on and, instead, of developing an alternative form of grip.

Tip: Do your best to work with gravity, rather than against it.

Note taking while walking around. For this protocol, you abandon your original position and work while standing or walking. You can walk up and down the room, visit the toilet, etc. This helps with the production of additional self-alignment possibilities once you have returned to your lying down position.

In addition to that, you can use the time to make written notes, draw sketches, etc., which you can draw upon for hints at the end of the overall summing up in your reporting session.

Standing. Stand up straight with your feet a shoulder width apart and your back straight but not strained. Don't make any effort to outwardly maintain your position without making any movement.

Marking your boundaries L. A precise assessment takes place in the lying down position, of where the "alien" and "home" begin and continue on. While doing it you begin at first with the body. The relevant areas are then also extended, as the case may be. In the note taking and reporting phases, the results are then documented in a schematic and graphic sketch.

PROTOCOL CHAPTER 8-4

00.00–00.40 (40') *Phase 1:* Lying down

00.40–01.15 (35') Phase 2: Orienting yourself by your avoidance direction

01.15–01.25 (10') *Phase 3*: Lying down

01.25–02.10 (45') *Phase 4*: Systematic pressure point change

02.10–02.30 (20') *Phase 5*: Note taking while walking around

02.30–02.35 (5') *Phase 6*: Lying down

02.35–02.45 (10') *Phase 7*: Picking up/putting down 100%

02.45–02.53 (8') *Phase 8*: Picking up/putting down 50%

02.53–03.01 (8') *Phase 9*: Picking up/putting down 25%

03.01–03.09 (8') *Phase 10*: Picking up/putting down 10%

03.09–03.30 (21') *Phase 11*: Note taking while walking around

03.30–03.55 (25') *Phase 12:* Systematic pressure point change

03.55–04.40 (45') *Phase 13*: Shallow breathing

04.40–05.05 (25') *Phase 14*: Lying down

05.05–06.05 (60') *Phase 15*: Report

Explanations

Lying Down. On your back (if necessary slightly skewed to the right), outwardly motionless, alert.

Orienting yourself by your avoidance direction. In the lying down position, determine your current overall body direction (e.g., the situation as determined by gravity) and immediately just on the impulse level, meaning without making any outward movement, turn in the other direction. If this is successful, then take a bearing once again upon the currently opposing direction on the impulse level, and so on.

Systematic pressure point change

While lying down, define five points on the body:

> *Right heel*
> *Left heel*
> *Right shoulder*
> *Left shoulder*
> *The middle of the back of your head*

Over the course of the protocol place your attention first upon pressure point 1 (right heel). This body point is to be determined precisely. Once this has happened (or your attention loosens or you find it starts wandering), change it over to pressure point 2 (left heel). Do the same thing here, until the pressure point has either been precisely determined and narrowed down or your attention lets go or wanders. Then direct your attention towards pressure point 3 (right shoulder) and continue proceeding accordingly. Pressure point 4 (left shoulder) follows, and then pressure point 5 (the middle of the back of your head). Once you have done all you can at pressure point 5, direct your attention back towards pressure point 1, and the cycle begins anew.

Note: It is important to make sure that when determining the pressure points you don't treat them imaginatively (be it as an image or abstractly in your mind), but as tangible objects, which you can define with your senses!

Note taking while walking around. For this protocol, you abandon your original position and work while standing or walking. You can walk up and down the room, or visit the toilet, etc. This helps with the production of additional self-alignment possibilities once you have returned to your lying down position.

   In addition to that, you can use the time to make written notes, draw sketches, etc., which you can draw upon for hints at the end of the overall summing up in your reporting session.

1. *Picking up/putting down 100 percent.* Move an object around in various ways; rearrange it, twist it around, put it away, etc. Carry this out initially at normal speed, to maintain a (subjective) reference value of 100 percent speed.

2. *Picking up/putting down 50 percent.* Just like point one, but with one half the speed (50 percent) in relation to the previously established reference value.

3. *Picking up/putting down 25 percent.* Just like point one, but with one-quarter the speed (25 percent) in relation to the previously established reference value.

You can proceed accordingly with further percentage figures. (So, 10 percent means 10 percent of the speed, always in comparison to the previously established reference value, and so on.)

Shallow breathing. Make your breathing as shallow as possible in the lying down position, without becoming tense.

General Overview of the Protocol Techniques

Walking a short space using impulsing. This consists of two sub-phases (1.1 and 1.2) as follows.

Sub-phase 1.1—Preparation (30'): Determine a spot that's three or four paces away from where you are and then mark it. Try walking it out once and then remove the mark.

Sub-phase 1.2—Main Part (90'): Starting from a lying down position, leave the place you are in without any external movement (see Impulse Circulation) and take the steps you decided upon in sub-phase 1.1. Then return again to your starting position and lie down, and then stand up again immediately, walk that stretch, etc.

Note: As the walking a short space using an impulsing protocol is accomplished *without any external movement,* it takes place just on the levels of motoric impulse. You must ensure that this is *not* just an act of imagining (be it as an image or abstractly in your mind), but a genuine physical (although purely "internal") impulsing!

Pressure empowerment 100 percent. In an upright position, legs a shoulder width apart, clasping an object in both hands and holding it clear in front of your body, without being supported by anything. This is first of all carried out with normal pressure, to maintain a (subjective) reference value of 100% expenditure of pressure.

You can proceed accordingly with further percentage figures. (So, 10 percent means 10 percent of pressure expenditure, always in comparison to the previously established reference value, and so on.)

It is recommended that you should use as the object perhaps an unbreakable plastic bottle filled with fresh water, which has been tightly closed beforehand. This will help in the event of letting the object slip and will avoid broken shards and resultant injuries as well as other damage.

It will turn out that over time the bottle will threaten to slip out of your hands. In fact, the use of a "deep grip" (that is, by using an ever stronger pressure) will also not permanently stop this process. ("In the depths, the grip gets lost.") For that reason, it's a matter of abandoning pressure exertion if possible when you are holding on and, instead, of developing an alternative form of grip.

Tip: Do your best to work *with* gravity rather than against it.

Shallow breathing. Make your breathing as shallow as possible in this lying down position, without becoming tense.

1. *Flat walking 100 percent.* Cover a determined distance at a normal walking pace. This is to be carried out initially with a normal downward pressure of the soles of the feet, in order to determine the (subjective) reference value of full pressure expenditure.

2. *Flat walking 50 percent.* Like 1, but with half the downward pressure (50 percent) in comparison with the previously established reference value.

3. *Flat walking 33 percent.* Like 1, but with one-third the downward pressure (33 percent) in comparison with the previously established reference value.

You can proceed accordingly with further percentage figures. (So, 10 percent means ten percent pressure expenditure, always in comparison to the previously established reference value, and so on.)

Tip: Take care to work *with* gravity instead of against it.

Marking your boundaries L. A precise assessment takes place in the lying down position, of where the "alien" and "home" begin and continue on. While doing it, you begin at first with the body. The relevant areas are then also extended, as the case may be. In the note taking and reporting phases, the results are then documented in a schematic and graphic sketch.

Marking your boundaries S. A precise assessment takes place in the lying down position, of where the "alien" and "home" begin and continue on. While doing it you begin at first with the body. The relevant areas are then also extended, as the case may be. In the note taking and reporting phases, the results are then documented in a schematic and graphic sketch.

Greater mudra. In a sitting position, let your upper arms rest gently against your torso. Touch the fingertips of both hands (so all ten fingers, i.e., including the thumbs) gently against each other, thus forming pairs. Then first of all reduce the pressure between the fingers of one pair, and next let it go completely, while still maintaining the contact between them. Eventually, carry out the same procedure with four fingertips, thus two further pairs, until at the end all the fingertips are still resting against each other, but without expending any pressure.

Should the fingertips become separated from each other, you must start the greater mudra all over again.

Note: You should make sure that this does *not* become a matter of imagining (whether it's figurative or abstract/mental) but instead that it's a genuine bodily and sensation-based operation.

Impulse circulation. Standing up *without any outward body movement* with an immediate return to a lying down position before any bodily reaction occurs.

Note: As impulse circulation is accomplished *without any external movement,* it takes place just on the levels of motoric impulse. You must ensure that this is *not* a matter of an act of imagining (be it as an image or abstractly in your mind), but a genuine physical (although purely "internal") impulsing!

Lesser mudra 1. In a sitting position, rest your upper arms against the sides of your body, and touch the tips of one pair of fingers (e.g., your index fingers) gently against each other. Then first of all reduce the pressure between the fingers, next let it go completely, while still maintaining the contact between them.

Should the fingertips become separated from each other, you must start the lesser mudra all over again.

Note: You should make sure that this does *not* become a matter of imagining (whether it's figurative or abstract/mental) but instead that it's a genuine bodily and sensation-based operation.

Lesser mudra number… See above. The numbers are there to indicate how many pairs of fingers to work with. With the number 2 that means two pairs (the index and ring fingers for example), with the number 3, three, and with the number 4, four pairs of fingers. No thumbs are used!

Collision empowerment. To be carried out in three sub-phases:

Sub-phase 1.1—Deciding on an object: Pick an immobile object and take up a standing position a few steps away from it.

Sub-phase 1.2—Align yourself towards a collision point, 100% distance away: Keeping your stance outwardly motionless, align yourself towards a collision with the object. You should ensure that this does *not* become a matter of imagination (whether it's figurative or abstract/mental), but instead that it's a genuine, inner-body, motoric process! Once the collision arc has been completely dealt with on a subjective basis, continue on to the next sub-phase.

Sub-phase 1.3—Align yourself towards a collision point, now 50 percent distance away: Reduce by half your distance away from the object. Then carry out the same procedure as described under 1.2.

Once you have exhausted the last sub-phase, perform the procedure as above with a different object.

Orienting yourself by your avoidance direction. In the lying down position, determine your current overall body direction (e.g., the situation as determined by gravity) and immediately just on the impulse level, meaning without making any outward movement, turn in the other direction. If this is successful, then take a bearing once again upon the currently opposing direction on the impulse level, and so on.

Note taking while walking around. For this protocol, you abandon your original position and work while standing or walking. You can walk up and down the room, or visit the toilet, etc. This helps with the production of additional self-alignment possibilities once you have returned to your lying down position.

In addition to that, you can use the time to make written notes, draw sketches etc., which you can draw upon for hints at the end of the overall summing up in your reporting session.

Steering fingers. Write by hand on an 8½-by-11-inch piece of paper for up to 30 minutes, eyes closed, on a theme of your own choosing.

Lying down. On your back (if necessary slightly skewed to the right), outwardly motionless, alert.

Impulsing in circular phases. An alternation between lying down and/or sleeping, and activities done while standing up, divided into phases. The latter can be performed using any activities you like, and the digits following indicate the value in minutes of the particular phases (5/5 = five minutes sleep/ five minutes standing up, etc.).

1. *Report.* The Report is carried out immediately straight after the end of the complete set of protocols, following a short break of five minutes maximum, which can be used for going to the bathroom, stretching your arms and legs, and so on. Everything must be written down and the time is divided into two parts.

2. The *Factual Report.* Here you make a list of all the events and of your observations, in order to hold on to them. This can be done in the form of keywords, simple sketches, etc. The Factual Report should always be carried out as comprehensively as possible.

3. The *Continuation of the Report*. Here thoughts, ideas, associations, detailed graphic sketches, questions, etc., are examined and clarified, with the aim of arriving at worthwhile conclusions and outcomes, as well as questions that will lead you on further.

Sitting. In a seated position, rest your feet flat on the floor, your legs not touching each other, and your back is in a comfortable upright posture, without leaning on the back of the chair. Your effort is focused on keeping your position outwardly completely motionless.

Standing. Stand up straight with your feet a shoulder width apart and your back straight but not strained. Don't make any effort to outwardly maintain your position without making any movement.

1. *Picking up/putting down 100%*. Move an object around in various ways; rearrange it, twist it around, put it away, etc. Carry this out initially at normal speed, to maintain a (subjective) reference value of 100 percent speed.

2. *Picking up/putting down 50 percent*. Just like point one, but with one half the speed (50 percent) in relation to the previously established reference value.

3. *Picking up/putting down 33 percent*. Just like point one, but with one third the speed (33 percent) in relation to the previously established reference value.

You can proceed accordingly with further percentage figures. (So, 10 percent means 10 percent of the speed, always in comparison to the previously established reference value, and so on.)

Systematic Pressure Point Change
While lying down, define five points on the body:

> *Right heel*
> *Left heel*
> *Right shoulder*
> *Left shoulder*
> *The middle of the back of your head*

Over the course of the protocol, place your attention first upon pressure point 1 (right heel). This body point is to be determined precisely. Once this has happened (or your attention loosens or you find it starts wandering), change it over to pressure point 2 (left heel). Do the same thing here, until the pressure point has either been precisely determined and narrowed down or your attention lets go or wanders. Then direct your attention towards pressure point 3 (right shoulder) and continue proceeding accordingly. Pressure point 4 (left shoulder) follows, and then pressure point 5 (the middle of the back of your head). Once you have done all you can at pressure point 5, direct your attention back towards pressure point 1, and the cycle begins anew.

Note: It is important to make sure that when determining the pressure points you don't treat them imaginatively (be it as an image or abstractly in your mind), but as tangible objects, which you can define with your senses!

Technical sleep. The aim here is to cross over directly into the sleep state without a transitional stage ("a gradual darkening," etc.). It is to be expected that this (initially) won't be successful, but if so one should continue to make an unbroken effort to get closer to it.

Orienting yourself by your avoidance direction. In the lying down position, determine your current overall body direction (e.g., the situation as determined by gravity) and immediately just on the impulse level, meaning without making any outward movement, turn in the other direction. If this is successful, then take a bearing once again upon the currently opposing direction on the impulse level, and so on.

Forest Walk 1 (Centralizing your effort)

A previously determined, tried and tested woodland path is followed at nighttime at a subjectively normal pace. At the same time a (likewise subjective) reference value of 100 percent speed as well as 100 percent downward pressure (through the soles of the feet) is determined. After one-third of the total distance, reduce the walking speed to half (50 percent), and after the second third reduce it again to 33 percent of the original walking pace. In parallel with that, also reduce the downward pressure to 50 percent and 33 percent, respectively.

It is admissible to illuminate your path occasionally and for a short period of time using a flashlight or something similar to avoid accidents, but this should be kept down to the bare minimum and only done where really necessary.

FOREST WALK 2 (GHOST STEP)

A previously determined, tried and tested woodland path is followed at nighttime divided into various sub-phases as follows.

Sub-phase 2.1—Weight displacement equalization (30'): While making a stride, initially put your center of gravity completely over the leading foot. Then, after a short pause, relocate it—with as little impetus as possible—to a position above the following foot. After a short pause while you transfer the pressure, move the following foot forward again, and so on.

Sub-phase 2.2—Striding (70'): Walk the next section of the track at a calm pace. While doing so, keep your attention as exclusively as possible upon your own sequence of movement. External distractions should be registered as seamlessly and as free from reflection as possible, without having a negative effect on you keeping your attention upon your walking.

Sub-phase 2.3—Weight displacement equalization (20'): Like 2.1.

Sources

Frater U.·.D.·. *High Magic. Theory and Practice.* Llewellyn Publications, Woodbury, MN. 2005.

———. *High Magic II. Expanded Theory and Practice.* Llewellyn Publications, Woodbury, MN. 2008.

———. *Money Magic: Mastering Prosperity in Its True Element.* Llewellyn Publications, Woodbury, MN. 2011.

Staudenmaier, Ludwig. *Magic as Experimental Science* (Only available in German as *Die Magie als experimentelle Naturwissenschaft*, Leipzig, 1912). Book version of 1910 in the Annals of Natural Philosophy, vol. 9 (1910), pp 329–367, published as an essay. An extended edition appeared in Leipzig in 1922.

International Contact Details for the Systema Martial Arts School

Vladimir Vasiliev
137 Birch Ave
Richmond Hill, Ontario
Canada – L4C 6C5
Tel: (905) 886-0483
Fax: (905) 886-7071
Email: training@russianmartialart.com
Web: www.russianmartialart.com/schoollocator.php

The Thanatos Meditation Object

Hagen von Tulien (born in Berlin on May 2, 1961) is a German artist and occultist living in Berlin, Germany. Building on more than thirty years of intensive experience with magical theory and practice, he has specialized in both giving expression to and also manifesting magical states of consciousness using art as a creative medium, as well as creating suitable tools for its spiritual application.

He has had an engagement with (and in some cases membership of) various orders and societies in the Eastern and Western magical traditions, including AMORC, the OTO, Thee Temple ov Psychick Youth (TOPY), Illuminates of Thanateros (IOT), Fraternitas Saturni, Société Voudon Gnostique (S.V.G.), and others. In addition, he was ordained as a bishop in the Ecclesia Gnostica Spiritualis by Michael Bertiaux.

You can request the "Thanatos Meditation Object" using the contact details below. Please bear in mind that availability might be limited.

Email: hagen93@online.de
Web: www.behance.net/Hagen_von_Tulien
      www.facebook.com/hagen.von.tulien